PRAISE

The blessing of the Almighty Father, Son, Holy Spirit is upon Rita. As I prayed for her God said, "you have gone where I have called you and Jesus says thank you. Thank you that you have done everything I have wanted you to do. Thank you that I said come and you came. Thank you that I said heal and you did healing. Thank you that I said set them free and you set them free." You are a modern-day Moses and the glory of God is falling on you. The Lord has anointed you and He is saying to you, your work has only just begun. The best is yet to come... I am delighted and honored to support Rita any way I can.

Cannon Andrew White, The Vicar of Baghdad

A moving personal account of one woman's story from childhood through adulthood chronicling the heartbreak and pain of physical, sexual and emotional abuse. It is not just a story of devastation and loss, but one of perseverance, healing and the triumph of God's grace. Rita illuminates to us the truths she encountered that Jesus deeply wove through the tattered threads of her life to re-create a beautiful tapestry of hope, healing, and restoration. I am grateful that she chose to courageously share her story with such candor, simplicity and humility. In so doing, she gives voice to the silent agony of many women, wives and daughters. It is a worthwhile read for all of us!

I recommend you take the time to read it, whether your story shares similarities or not, you will encounter Truth that leads to freedom, and gain understanding for the pain that many women carry as a result of the trauma of abuse in their lives. May you find hope and courage to believe that you deserve to be whole, loved, healed and free. May you encounter the great grace of Jesus Christ who came to set us free! I certainly did as I read through these pages.

Pastor Amy Bailey, The Stirring

I am happy to say Rita has journeyed many times through the valley of the shadow and emerged with a victory found in her relationship to Jesus. If you need encouragement or a pathway to a victorious life this book will be a light to your path.

DOUGLAS N PORTER M.A. LMFT

Leaving
the Lie

A story of freedom from trauma

Rita Renee Davis

RevivALL Publishing

REDDING, CALIFORNIA

Unless otherwise marked, Scripture quotations are taken from The Passion Translation. Copyright © by Passion & Fire Ministries, Inc. Used by permission. All rights reserved.

Scripture quotations marked NKJ are taken from the New King James Version®. Copyright © 1982 by Thomas Nelson. Used by permission. All rights reserved.

Cover photo: Zephaniah Appel, IG @Zephapple

Cover design: Robert Henslin – www.rhdcreative.com

Interior design and editing: Rich Bullock – www.perilousfiction.com

Published by RevivALL Publishing, USA

V 07/12/23

This book is dedicated to two of my Heavenly supporters:

To my grandmother, "Grandma Goose." For being the matriarchal catalyst in my faith, teaching me what it meant to be a woman of God, a mighty prayer warrior, and setting the foundation in which to build my home. You were there when I took my first breath, and I was there when you took your last. I miss you so much.

To auntie Beni Johnson, for being a constant in my life. You saw me for who I was underneath the pain and brokenness. You nurtured the original design and inspired me to continue to tell my story. Thank you for being such a maternal figure in my life, full of faith and intercession. I miss you so much.

CONTENTS

FOREWORD

BY BILL JOHNSON

You're about to read the story of a champion. And while it would be appropriate to celebrate and honor the author for her courage and willingness to follow Jesus in the worst of situations, the champion is Jesus. Again. Only Jesus. He is the healer of brokenness and the forgiver of the sins that plague our hearts. He alone could turn this nightmare into His dream.

Only the Father's redemptive solution can create a Christ-like identity in us that can withstand the perils of our day. But the solutions are not found through religious hype, or the intense strain of trying to get it right. They are found in truth. And truth is a person. It's His truth that sets us free: free from our past, from an unhealthy world-view, and from the lies we've believed. The author brilliantly identifies those lies. And then through her personal story, she dismantles each lie to bring the reader face to face with the goodness of God.

I get so encouraged hearing and seeing the stories of how our Father brings life and healing to impossible situations. And while I love it when the miracles of Scripture happen in people's bodies, right before our eyes, it's the transformation of a life that thrills me most. This book, *Leaving the Lie*, is about just that.

In measure, my wife, Beni, and I have had a front-row seat to Rita's journey. Beni loved her so deeply. We have both been profoundly moved by Rita and Cody's courage to let Jesus do what only He can do, which always involves surrender. There is no progress in the life of a believer apart from surrender, and surrender always leads to trust. For God, our perfect heavenly Father, is completely trustworthy.

This is a story of great grace. And even if your life was never riddled with the types of sins of Rita's past, it was still marked by sin. For all of us need a savior. Regardless of our past, God will use this story to bring life to each reader.

I believe that God will use this book to bring strength to the weak, hope to the hopeless, and deliverance to the bound. Put on your seatbelts as you enter the story of a perfect Father embracing the impossibilities of a broken life, until those broken things testify of the goodness and greatness of God.

Bill Johnson
Bethel Church, Redding, CA
Author of *God is Good* and *Power of Communion*
(co-authored with Beni Johnson)

INTRODUCTION

"Call to me and I will answer you and tell you great and hidden things you do not know." Jeremiah 33:3

I live in the country on six acres. Since the day I moved in, I began building a pathway. I call it Gethsemane, meaning "oil press." A pathway in my yard that signifies and reminds me of the crushing hours of Christ's suffering on our behalf.

Along the pathway you will find many treasures I have collected since I was a little girl, treasures of pendants, wood pieces, shells, iron, and other symbolic items of places, things, and people throughout my life. I placed the treasures with care along a dry riverbed of peppered stone.

Every year, every inch of this pathway becomes overgrown with weeds. One sunny afternoon in late January, I was hunched over pulling weeds—my hands sore and my back aching from intensely digging between the crevices of rock. I assessed what work lie ahead. It was covered in weeds and I had only just begun. My head spun, alone in this daunting task.

The callous and harsh reality hit me. This was a picturesque analogy of what my life had been, and then the weeds started appearing to me as painful acts of trauma proliferating in the lives of not just me, but people everywhere. I began sobbing uncontrollably. I needed to do something.

With fury, I pulled them out of the ground, crying out for His tender mercy. Bleeding, dirty, scraped up, bruised, and beaten, I raised my hands to Him. A gust of wind blew all around me in one swift motion, and then stopped. I rested in the peace as a beam of warm sunshine lay on my face giving me comfort—the same warm beam that had shown up so many times before. God whispered to me, "Leave The Lie."

I opened my eyes and looked down at the pathway. This time there were only a few weeds. I gently tugged at them, each one releasing with ease out of the moist earth. God met me there in a great symbolic manner on the pathway of Gethsemane.

On my own, it was painful, overwhelming, and my perspective was askew. With God, I was given peace and comfort, and in that I was able to extract each weed with ease. With every pull, the daunting task shrank.

Without God, the lies I carried were overwhelming, and with Him, we pulled every lie from my past. God stayed with me the rest of that day, and together we walked through every old lie. Together, we celebrated the testimony of life and the truth that I carry. He nourished the truth in me until I found complete freedom.

I remain steadfast in this journey until I am the original design of who I was created to be. Sharing my story is a continuum of my healing and a catalyst for healing others. Our stories are the nutrients for the harvest of many.

For those reading this book, I want to pray for you.

I want you to know, you are seen. You may feel so lost right now and it hurts. But you are a survivor, an overcomer. Be who you need to be to get through it.

You are not what people have done to you, you are a child of the Almighty King. Turn towards God, surrender it all and wipe off the shame the world has tried to place on you, releasing every toxic thing at His feet. God will move in your life, liberated, authentic, and pure.

Father, I pray for the person holding this book. Against the many things that have come to try and kill, steal or destroy their healing process.

I pray that they are seen and loved. That they receive support and friendship in the most surprising and utmost loyal ways.

I pray that trust is restored through Holy Spirit and against isolation during times they want to retreat or pretend nothing has happened.

I pray above all that God's voice is clear so that you can hear only His words and walk-in obedience to complete restoration.

I pray that this book inspires the one and that they can receive the healing that they so deserve to walk in their truth. Amen."

– Rita Renee

THE LIE: IT NEVER HAPPENED

"Even when bad things happen to the good and godly ones, the Lord will save them and not let them be defeated by what they face." Psalm 34:19

CIRCA 1987, I WAS 12 YEARS OLD. I stayed after school several days a week to help our music teacher on the set of an upcoming play. I loved every aspect of theatre: stepping outside of myself, challenging my imagination, and becoming the creator of things in ways I could never imagine. When not trying out for a role in a play, I was volunteering on set, creating and building with other students. It was the highlight of my junior high years.

Many perceived me as a shy young girl, even a little insecure, but this wasn't the case at all. I chose all my friends wisely. The friends I connected with released the extrovert in me. I was unstoppable around them. Something I still carry to this day.

One day, the music teacher in charge of theatre, asked if I would volunteer alone on set. We only needed one person on the finishing touches of the set. The bell rang, signaling the end of the school day. I gathered my things, threw my arms around a couple of good friends, and wished them well as I took off toward the theatre inside the gymnasium. Laughter and excitement filled the hallways as I walked to the gymnasium located across from the school office. I opened the big door and stepped inside. I stood there, looking around the large room. The door slammed shut, startling me as the enormous boom echoed in the room.

I walked up the steps toward the back of the stage. There was a single chair, a couple pieces of wood, and paint. I stood there for a moment. Something felt different. I picked up the paintbrush, knelt down, and began painting. The door banged again. I didn't jump this time. It had to be the music teacher. I prepared myself and the things around me, expecting to receive acknowledgement of work well done.

As expected, he showed up with a warm smile and a multitude of affirmations. At one point, he asked me to step back and admire it all with him. I quickly got up off the floor and stepped to his side. He pulled the single chair back a little and sat in it while staring at the creative work and describing his vision for the stage setting and some things that needed to be completed. He then affirmed me, telling me how proud of me he was for helping him get things done. I felt very appreciated and for my efforts.

I was beautifully innocent, a little Pollyanna in a small town. I lived on a short block of five homes surrounded by pastures. My sisters and I loved hanging out with the neighborhood kids. Our tiny community was a place where we could play until dark or until our mothers called us home. Sometimes after a day of work, my dad would turn the corner in his truck we called "old blue." All the kids would pile on top of the hood, the roof, or the back of the truck, and he would drive us all slowly home.

On sunny weekends, dad would pile hay bales up to the top of old blue, then he drive them to the four corners of the field across the street and we would build mazes out of them. The mazes led us to a treehouse, where we held secret meetings and talked for hours about nothing. During the rainy seasons, the field flooded, and we would drag out the neighbor's old wooden fishing boat and row it across the small patch of floodwater over to the tree fort. It was one of my favorite places outside of school and my home.

My parents designed and built our home—a long-awaited dream after living in a small one-bedroom trailer with the five of us. We each had our own room. My room was pink, filled with posters that told stories of hope filled dreams, fashion, young love, and music. I spent as much time in my room as I did in those old hay mazes. My creativity and imagination ran wild—uninhibited—in the privacy of my own room.

My parents were a vital part of the local church we attended, and both served in leadership positions. Youth group was also one of my favorite places. This gave me my first sense of what family belonging was outside of my home. Between home and church, the world was one big fun adventure—a safe environment to express myself and be who I wanted to be without judgment or fear. Life was pure, free, and wildly adventurous. Even if something bad was going on, I don't think my heart would have accepted it.

My parents were both firm in their discipline. I knew exactly what lines I could cross and which ones I should not. Now and then, it was worth the trouble to cross that line. However, my parents raised me to honor and respect authority, and the consequence of disrespecting authority was harsh and sometimes included spanking. This was a line I was never willing to cross.

The music teacher encompassed all things of authority to me. He was a father, a husband, and my teacher. My current life experience, combined with his authority, created within me a place that swelled with honor and respect. So when he asked me to have a seat on his lap in the chair, I trusted him.

I also felt fear.

Something deep inside of me let out a blood-curdling scream, a sort of siren. I had never felt trust and fear in the same room. It was uncomfortable, it scared me. It was fear itself that drew me to sit on his lap, but it was his lap that would ultimately lead to captivity. He moved his hands down my thighs patting the side of my bottom and then over the top and slightly in between. I jumped up.

As if nothing happened, he looked over at the woodpile and said in a matter-of-fact tone that we needed more wood.

"Let's take a ride up to the house and get it."

I agreed. Anything to get me out of that room and away from the fear I was feeling.

We walked in silence to his truck. He opened the door, and I sat down. As we drove up the road to his house, I tried to create a sense of normalcy through small talk. By the time we approached his house at the top of a hill, I had rationalized my racing thoughts to a peaceful place. The view was spectacular, and his home was full of windows. We sat in the truck; I couldn't seem to move. He pointed to the house and said, "*I built the inside staircase. Would you like to come in and see it?*"

I have no recollection of what happened after that moment. The next thing I remembered was walking down the road toward my house from the school. Our home was about nine blocks from the school, making it an extremely easy walk home. Many neighborhood kids would meet up along the way, and it gave us all a sense of independence. We had no cell phones then, so we decided before school that day or days in advance how I would get home. I had told my parents my intent to walk home that day.

The road had a bit of an incline and ran alongside a little creek. I was feeling spacey and scared, grasping for memories of the day. I was painting. I was walking to a truck. I was painting. I got in the truck. Oh yes! I went to his home. Did I go in? How did I get here?

With every attempt at remembering, I became anxious, and fear of being alone crept up. I began talking to myself to fill the void. I veered to the right side of the road, near the creek, hoping to find peace. The wind scattered leaves along my path, and the creek trickled along the rocks. How did I get here? How did I get here? *How did I get here?!*

Closing my eyes, I let out a slight whimper and then looked up. There was a man lying upside down alongside the creek. He appeared disheveled and homeless. He looked dead. Was he breathing? I was terrified and yelled out to wake him. He was lifeless, and so in a panic, I fell back in the gravel and scooted myself backwards up the embankment toward the road.

Once reaching the edge of the road, I stood up and took a couple steps toward the creek again, looking for the man. I stretched forward, using the tree line as a barricade, and peered through the trees. He was gone. My chest tightened, making it hard to breathe. Was this man even real or had something happened in the lost time that opened a portal to demons? My thoughts ran away with me down the road and through the field toward my home—and right into my pink room.

I woke up to the smell of hamburger meat and the sweet melody of

Beethoven. The piano sat up against the wall between the kitchen and the dining room. My mom always played while she cooked dinner. Dad sat atop one of the kitchen chairs with a newspaper in his hands, briefly pulling it down to share one of his jokes. My sisters did homework at the table, arguing and competing for Dad's attention. It all felt normal.

I walked down the hall into the kitchen and plopped myself at the counter.

Dad said, "Hey, nasal"—his nickname for me a long running family joke.

"Hi, dad."

He asked me how school was, and if I was going to be staying after again. Something happened in me during the moment he asked that, shaking me out of normalcy and into a new space created for me.

This space was like a room in my head. It wasn't too open, where I would feel vulnerable, and never too small, where I felt panic. The room was high above everything. It had a window I could peek out and look down on any moment. No one could see or hear me, but I was able to assess all that was going on.

I do not know what I said, how I looked, or what happened in that very moment, but my response caused the room to shift. From my space, I saw the way my parents looked at each other, the anger rising in my dad. With one look, they knew. Soon, there were tears, phone calls to teachers, and discussions. Then, it was if it never happened. Whatever transpired that day fragmented into pieces.

I have only two vivid memories of that day: the moment before I was running home, and the moments after. Whatever happened in the missing time was a deep, hidden wound. I was a secret sufferer. NeitherI did not have all the answers, so I doubted my own memory. I wanted to believe it never happened, but could not excuse the silent effects the unresolved trauma had on my life.

Throughout the years, this distant memory would creep back into my life, affecting everything around me. I began self-doubting any relationship, even my *perception* of that relationship. Any type of safe foundation built with another would crumble.

The first time this happened, I was about 19 years old. I was at a bridal shower, sitting at a table with a group of friends. We were headed down memory lane when someone brought up the teacher's name. My mind began going into a state of shock.

My heart was beating vigorously, my blood pulsing with adrenaline. The familiar fear crept back into my space—very much like the time at the creek when I saw the man lying dead. Like a bottomless whirlpool, I was sucked into fear. The voices were distant, and I knew I was going to my safe place, disassociating. I pleaded with myself to come back. I wanted to hear what they were saying.

Just as fast as it started, I was back in my chair, listening to the conversation. Afraid of leaving again, I blurted out, "Did he ever touch any of you?" Not wanting to expose myself, I finished the question off with, "I heard," and "maybe it *is* rumors." I remember one of my friends saying she heard another girl had been inappropriately touched, but it was never confirmed. The irony of that night was—even though this was the first moment when I did not feel alone—I was still believing nothing had happened.

The second time, I was in my early twenties, walking down the street alone. A man in the distance walked toward me, and I recognized it was the teacher. Again, my mind and body reacted in panic. This time, I felt like I was going to throw up. I started to yell out loud to myself, *"Pull it together!"* What was I supposed to do?

There were many options racing through my mind. Run across the street? Dip and duck into a nearby store? Pretend you don't see him and keep walking by? NO! The moment had come so quickly, he was standing before me. I stopped. Yelling out, "I know what you did!" He looked at me very puzzled and continue by. Leaving me full of more doubt than ever before.

The third time, I was in my late twenties, and my baby sister was in school. I found out he was her teacher. Even in the doubt, even in the lack of memory, even when I wanted to keep up with the lie that nothing happened, I found myself so full of rage at the very thought of him still teaching. If it weren't for the possibility he could hurt my sister, I would never have found the courage or strength to file a police report. I came with my doubt-filled story and laid out the *beginning* and the *end* of my memory—for the chance another student may have a *middle* piece to her story. I prayed this would never happen, but if it did, and if there was a report with the mention of his name, it would help her.

Repressed memory is one of the most controversial topics in psychology. Wikipedia states it is "largely scientifically discredited." The American Psychological Association states that it is not possible to distinguish repressed memories from false ones without corroborating evidence, rising the term Dissociative Amnesia in the DSM-V. Dissociative Amnesia is defined as the inability to recall autobiographical information. [1]

These types of terms and controversies from professionals, along with the social stigma from peers, created a barrier between what I felt— which was pain and trauma and the truth which I sought. I believed that there was no one to talk to, and I hated it. Why did what I went through have to be identified through study, professional or profession, or diagnostic and definition, for it to be real? Why did what I went through become a mental health disorder, instead of a community of people coming together through mercy and compassion and guiding me into health through belonging and trust?

While society and professionals argued over their professional terms, I suffered alone. My mind had some hidden memory, whether real or imagined, that had a negative impact on my life. All these moments were so traumatizing. They combined with the responses of those I had trusted, and the lack of awareness and resources, and resulted in no useful truth to help facilitate my ultimate healing and restoration. This compounded the lie within me that it never happened.

I continued to live in that lie until I was 48 years old. Repressed trauma can create years of unresolved pain and destroy the system of discernment that lives within you. I was constantly at war with my thoughts, checking facts and questioning reality. I lived a dual life: one that suffered in silence and self-doubt, and one that overcompensated through loud and self-seeking behaviors, a false confidence. At a young age, I noticed the vicious cycle I was in. Would anyone believe me? Did I believe in myself? I was paranoid, and it affected my creative imagination. I lived on the fine line between reality and fantasy.

Before graduating eighth grade, I dropped out of theatre. However, living a life without theatre was oxymoronic, because I was performing one of the greatest act of all. I was not authentic regarding who I truly was, finding it easier to become someone who everyone could accept. The truest expressions of myself were hidden in the secret places of poetry and photography. The creative places that were unseen, buried in spaces where they could not be judged or questioned for their authenticity.

2

THE LIE: I AM FINE

*"There is no such thing as darkness with you. The night, to you,
is as bright as day; there's no difference between the two."*
Psalm 139:12

AT THE AGE OF 13, PURITY BECAME MY identity. I wore it like a bold outward statement, covering the potential for someone seeing anything otherwise. Purity was not just indicative of my sexuality, but it became the staple of who I was, whether clothing or music, how I spoke, or what television shows I watched. Part of staying on the continuum of this identity compelled me to join a youth group at a local church, and I stayed there until I graduated high school.

High school was a time of discovery and independence. I had a close-knit group of friends, and there were three of us within the group that were inseparable. They were my ride-or-die, the safety zone.

Friendship in the 1980s consisted of passing notes, Reebok shoes, gunny sack dresses, and feathered hair firmly held back by half a can of Aqua Net. Computers were barely a thing, and pagers ruled portable communication. Cruises, beach parties, football games, and dances were the way to meet cute guys outside of school. If you drank, smoked weed, or had sex under the age of seventeen, it was a great scandal. Going to high school in the late 80s brought a series of firsts, and there were a lot of firsts between us three girls.

We came from three vastly different upbringings. Each of us brought something different to the table, making it a curiously fun friendship. One night we were having a sleepover, and my friend said something about how she heard that smoking banana peels and ground coffee beans were a mild psychedelic. Not realizing that there was a process to it, we simply peeled a banana, placed wet coffee grounds on it and rolled it up into a blunt size to smoke it—with no outcome.

This was one moment among many that my friends and I would try out bizarre things. We were the group that snuck nude photos, watched soft sex scenes in movies during slumber parties, and practiced kissing our pillows—feeling safe to explore all the things I deeply wanted to know under the façade of purity.

I adopted purity somewhere between the sexual revolution and purity culture. It wasn't wrong to want it, but when it is completely wrapped up in who you are, it becomes a falsely rooted identity.

An identity in Christ is whole, healed, and purposeful. Rather than being shamed into purity, we can make a personal decision through developing a deep relationship with Jesus. Identity is not the thing in which we find pleasure or end up finding the people we enjoy sharing life with over time. It is not our passions or our hobbies, all of which are fleeting. When we are defined by things that change or grow in seasons, it can develop hopelessness, a false sense of joy, chaos, confusion, and this leads to death without life.

Dating or "crushing" on boys in the 80s had a level of innocence you see little of today because of the onset of technology. Without social media or cell phones, our interaction with boys was limited to one-on-one, dances, and football games. We wrote the crush of the week on our textbook covers and practiced last name changes.

When my friends began dating, I celebrated them through the guise of purity, while internally I was deeply wounded. The first date or first kiss my friends experienced seemed to emphasize my failure as a "normal" teen, which then spiraled into a world of insecurities.

All those insecurities developed the next lie: "I am fine." *I am fine* meant I would have to prove it to everyone. When you need to prove yourself to people, you set yourself up for an unhealthy need of approval.

The constant need for validation created multiple layers that covered up the ability to be vulnerable, to be truthful, and to build lasting and committed relationships. These layers were words—I wore each one like a fashion statement, wearing so many by the time I graduated, I was a slave to reputation and faux identity, lost in translation by allowing those around me to tell me who I was. If I slowed down to look at my reflection, I would see the words that I wore—words that emulated a pile of tattered and dirty hand-me-down rags.

Outside of my loyal girl group, I spent time with a plethora of guy friends. I thought boys were cute. But, if a guy showed signs he felt like that about me, I shut him down at once and put him in the friend zone.

This quickly drove me into being labeled as "tomboy," "tease," or "off limits." The boys in high school either became close friends or they would not approach me at all. For some boys, it was a conquest, which caused me to withdraw further inside myself out of fear of their disingenuousness—creating yet another layer. By age 14, I was insecure, distrustful, and in desperate need of validation.

In my junior year, I was asked to the prom for the first time. The phone rang, and it was a really popular student in our school, *Paul. We hardly knew each other, but I did know he was the most wanted boy in school.

The hierarchy status of students was quite real. Band, theatre, yearbook club, student council, and then sports at the top. I kind of bounced between all the groups, but I was not "popular." The cheerleading squad was the envy of the school, and a few of my best friends were on it. I tried out once, but did not make the team, and so I kept to myself.

Over time, my friends all became something within the hierarchy of high school. I painfully moved along, hiding beneath the layer of being *fine*. The senior cheerleader—and homecoming queen—also had her sights on Paul. She wanted to go to prom with him, but instead, he called me.

When he asked me, there was a blend of excitement and uncertainty in my *yes*. To move up in the popularity hierarchy, my sudden yes superseded all the discernment welling up inside me. Within minutes of saying it, another call came in from a trusted male friend of mine. He, too, invited me to the prom.

After I explained to him all that transpired, his defenses went up quickly, and he begged me to step away and go with him. At the time, it felt like he was meddling in my excitement. He must not want me to be happy, or maybe he was just jealous.

Instead of seeing the whole picture or hearing my friend out, my walls went up. If I had been healthy, trusted him, realized that he heard the "locker room talk," I would have understood he knew far more than I did. I told him, "I am fine," hung up, and pushed it all away.

Prom night finally came. They transformed the once familiar place of games and rallies into a dance floor with decorations hung far above my head. Lights were dim, and music played. Anticipatory laughter and conversation echoed through the room. Paul pulled me onto the dance floor.

Throwing his arms around me, he drew me in. My heart raced a million miles a minute. Once again, I found myself in a school gym with a guy who was drawing me in, pressing on me. I spiraled as he thrust his tongue in my face, and my mind landed somewhere between the safe space and the present moment. It was my first kiss.

He pulled away and smiled as I wiped my face, holding back tears. Was it a flashback, being in a gym with a guy trying to touch me? A projection of the past? Was it the ideal of purity? Or, was he a guy on a conquest? Regardless, I felt assaulted.

Sick to my stomach and full of fear, shame crept in, beating myself up over being disgusted with a kiss. Desperately wanting to feel normal, I carried on throughout the evening, hiding under the façade of being totally fine while he made several more advances toward me throughout the night. When the last dance came, I was physically relieved.

We headed toward the car to leave. There was excitement at the thought of being home. When he said he had a surprise for me, I obliged out fear that he would view me differently and report back to all my peers with stories that would invalidate me as a person. I had to keep my composure and ensure that I was fine for both myself and him.

He pulled out a rag and tied it snug around my eyes. The lies I had allowed to clothe me rendered me powerless in that moment. On the inside, I was screaming with fear. On the outside, I could not say a word, as if paralyzed.

When we arrived, he guided me out of the car and into a building. I heard a few distant voices in the background. Scuffing my feet, I found the floor flat but slightly soft, like a thin carpet. Realizing we were in a hotel, panic rose. I went to the safe space in my mind until hearing a familiar male voice. It was a trusted friend.

There was whispering, a bit of a tussle, and the friend asked if I was okay. Amidst the fear I uttered, "I am fine." But I wasn't fine—far from it. Somehow, this trusted friend knew something was wrong. He convinced everyone that we needed to go. Reminiscent of years ago, I suddenly found myself back home in my pink room.

Being fine was an unhealthy coping mechanism. It was a lie built out of necessity, a trauma response to triggers. The night of prom was a public crushing of the purity façade, exposing a multitude of insecurities and categorically becoming the reason I started to sabotage friendships around me.

If there was any indication that I was not fine, I would retreat into isolation, where I could secure myself in a first-rate plan of excellence. Isolation was the least plan of resistance, a place that lacked the motivation to move toward authenticity or truth.

Nearing the end of my senior year and losing friendships at a rapid rate, something kept tugging at me, telling me to prepare for a great and mighty battle. I was scared, feeling unprepared for any battle.

While my body matured, my thoughts and emotions lacked maturity. I was young, and the assaults on me slowed my progress and altered my emotional growth. Parts of me had become more grown up than they should have, and other parts were childlike, stunting my ability to process and respond to life in a mature manner.

My thoughts were on repeat, telling me I would never be ready for the world. I was completely lost. The lie, "I am fine," became a portal for the enemy to enter and have his way with me.

3

THE LIE: I AM NOT WORTHY

"And I find that the strength of Christ's explosive power infuses me to conquer every difficulty." Philippians 4:13

IN MY SENIOR YEAR, WHEN EVERYTHING hit all at once, it came with such high velocity it shifted the trajectory of my life and all cognitive responses. I was unprepared, and I did not understand.

First, it was youth group. My dad left the youth leadership role after years. I was not getting along with our senior youth pastor. There was a lot of tension and arguing with leadership, coupled with my desperate desire for validation. In it, I decided everyone was out to get me. The church was a filler for my fun, and when it wasn't fun anymore, I dropped out. Without community and high school relationships, I went deeper into isolation. Isolation translated to abandonment, and abandonment described my worth.

Next, my mom started a new job, and my parents sold the house we built. Mom's job consumed all her time, and after years of being at home, it was sort of a crossroads to full freedom for me, and another added element of abandonment. Moving out of our childhood home was devastating. The attachment I had to our home was so incredible that the day we moved, it was as if they ripped a limb from me, the pain excruciating.

In the midst of unrelenting life adjustments, my safe space was under siege. The enemy was gaining momentum, rendering me powerless in my feeble attempts to maintain the lies. Somewhere between war and survival, I missed the disconnect happening between my parents.

One day, Dad picked me up in his work van. I was sitting in the front seat watching the scenery slide by as we drove down the freeway. It was a sunny day, and there were yellow daisies everywhere. He pulled off the ramp near a field and turned off the engine. There was silence as we sat there, staring.

I thought nothing of it at first, since my dad and I are so much alike. Sitting quiet in our thoughts was something quite natural for us. But that day something felt horribly different as anxiousness filled the van.

My dad broke the silence abruptly with words that struck like lightning.

"Your mom and I are getting a divorce."

Did you know, when lightning strikes, it carries an enormous shock wave through your entire nervous system, causing permanent and sometimes fatal injuries? The strike from his words was near fatal; I lost complete control.

I had put every ounce of self-worth into the safety of my home environment. Once my parents pulled that out from under me, I had to confront the perceived reality that my life was a lie, church was a lie, my family was now a lie. Was God a lie too?

My parents were high school sweethearts. My mom lost her mother to cancer at a very young age. Her father was a highway patrolman. Even though my grandfather remarried, my mom and her two sisters maternally fended for themselves. My dad lost his father to a car accident as a child, leaving his mother to raise five children under the age of eight. Both my parents were raised up together, their siblings found friendship with each other. It seemed inevitable that they would find love.

They were 17 years old when they found out they were pregnant with me. Despite their lack of elation, the families gathered and urged my parents to accept full responsibility. By the age of 18, Mom and Dad were married.

Dad signed up for the military, which took him from California, where they grew up, to the state of Colorado. For the first time, they were both alone, with family states away.

I was very aware of their struggles, but even more aware of their willingness to put in the hard work for a family and marriage. There were days they found it difficult to buy bread, but both of them together strove for success.

By the age of 24, they had three children ages 6 and under. They built an entire life together right out of high school—a foundation built from morals and principles of the Bible. To me, they were a success story, and my admiration of them ran deep. Their marriage, their jobs, their church, and community involvement became the standard by which I set my own life.

My parents were together just under twenty years when the divorce became final. The blow of the split opened a portal to things unseen.

My parents weren't perfect.

Just after my graduation, I became very aware of alcohol in the house. I would come home and clean up a few empty bottles here and there, until it came to a point where I was rushing to beat my sisters home to pick up the bottles.

I knew something wasn't right when I had to remove a large whiskey bottle from the shower. I did not know who all the bottles belonged to, and I never asked.

In my upbringing, I had little experience with any lifestyle outside of church and home, which is why cleaning up the bottles became an automatic response to my lack of self-esteem, a sort of chore to imply I had value to add to the mess.

I know my parents wanted to make things work behind closed doors, but in the process, they unintentionally created family secrets, doubt, and fear. Within the walls of the new home, the spirit was tense. During the day, they touched each other less and less.

Dad's jokes turned to sarcasm, and mom's joy turned to disdain. Evenings were the hardest. Most of the time, I would curl up on my bed and just pray it away.

Things changed abruptly for me one day when I came home to find my mother on the floor lying up against the fireplace. She had an empty bottle in one hand, completely intoxicated, her arm wrapped around a woman who was also drunk. It hurt.

I wished it was my dad. That's exactly what I thought. It would have been so much easier for me to handle. My dad was strong and could bounce back, but my mom, she was the pillar, and I felt severely helpless to see her broken. I had placed all my worth on my family, and we were cracking at the seams.

At this point, I had convinced myself that I was completely unworthy of friendships, family, or community. I was attending junior college and became one of the football cheerleaders. They held me to a standard I could not (or did not know how to) attain. I was on my own and, without my family intact, I lacked the motivation and encouragement to keep showing up for school or cheer practice.

I met a few high school aged people who invited me to a house party. This age group was the safest I had felt. Having little to no trust in people, I was not ready for adulthood or college, and they provided attention without intimacy. I placed my worth at a surface level and, in order to keep it that way, I sat in the background, filling my inner void with noise and music. There was an occasional friendly hello, until eventually someone offered alcohol and weed.

The first time I got drunk was off a bottle of peach schnapps. I was at a house party, and I remember being very sick. Someone helped me to the bathroom, where I leaned against the tub and vomited profusely. People were continuously in and out, checking on me. I heard a loud banging on the door and a lot of scuffling. The cops were there!

Suddenly, a group came in and picked me up and carried me into a backroom closet. They threw in a small garbage can and shut the door on me. Scared, I tried to get up, but my body was numb from the alcohol, and every attempt to move caused my head to bang from one side of the closet to the other. It was nauseating, creating a convulsion of dry heaves. I promised myself never to drink peach schnapps again, and I never did. But the introduction to alcohol was a gateway to escaping pain, and so I kept on doing it after that night.

I quit college.

My home had one rule: no rent if you are in college or working full time. I was doing neither. I started coming home all hours of the night, and sometimes I wouldn't come home at all except for a shower. My dad gave me an ultimatum—I chose to leave.

Eighteen. I had no responsibilities and the freedom to make any choice I wanted. I got high and drank regularly. An alternate personality came out when I was intoxicated. She was invincible, and younger peers looked up to her. She was in charge of her life, funny, not afraid of anything—and valued.

My intoxicated personality took comfort in a friendship with a teenage boy. He was everything to me. My escape. My every thought and every moment. I poured everything I was and everything I had into him. But it would come at a cost.

I remember the night I lost my virginity. It was evening, and we were at a friend's house. The window was open, and chiffon drapes were blowing all around. Every hurt, every painful violation in my life, every lie, had brought me to that moment. I was willing to compromise everything I always wanted for my life because I felt unworthy of all the things I once believed. This moment was my truth. He was my only truth.

4

THE LIE: I AM UNSEEN

"The eyes of the Lord are toward the righteous and his ears toward their cry." Psalm 34:15

THE FIRST BREAKUP, AFTER LOSING MY virginity, was life altering.

When two people are intimate physically, the brain releases chemicals inducing physiological connection. A connection so intricate that, when it's severed, the body's entire system can break down, causing anxiousness, depression, and illness.[1]

When we broke up, I was in so much physical distress I responded in unnatural ways to release it, making desperate attempts to be near him by calling his parents and inviting myself over, or hanging out with his friends. I would ask where he was and show up in places where I would plead with him to take me back. His resistance caused me to panic.

It wasn't just physical for me; there was this inexplicable attachment that was so deeply spiritual. I was connected to another soul in some realm that I never knew existed, and I couldn't cope with any of it. I was lonely, had no home, and friends were a commodity.

I brought up my other personality indefinitely. She was the one everybody noticed, the one everyone wanted to be around. And, because she only came out when intoxicated, my drinking turned from nights, to all day, every day.

When intoxicated, I would pick up just about anyone who gave me attention and go home with them at the end of every night. If there was no one to go home with, I would stay in the back of my car and sob until I fell asleep, waking up and enduring the cycle all over again.

I was killing my spirit with every choice made—handing responsibility over to the men I slept with, as if they were to blame for every feeling of abandonment, hopelessness, insecurity, or shame. This went on for several years until I felt love toward someone: *Tom. It frightened me how quickly and hard I fell in love, I was afraid to trust in the love I felt. I wanted to hold onto it but it frightened me more to let it go.

With Tom, I defined love, claiming it as my own. I controlled what it looked like, shaping and shifting it into a vision board full of romantic adventures and a future of living together. When the vision would fail, I bowed to fear and blamed myself, demanding that my my other personality, the intoxicated one, rise to the occasion.

Tom was a strong and very independent man. I loved that. He motivated me to move independently. He opened his whole life to me, including his home. I wanted more. Under the guise of my idea of love, I felt seen.

He became my obsession, and I was on a quest to be perfect for him.

There was a moment early in our relationship when I was getting ready for a night out, standing in front of the mirror, in my bra and underwear, putting my makeup on. I was feeling my best. He walked through the room and smiled. I smiled back. Then he smacked me on the butt and said, "You have a cottage cheese ass." Those words were a stone to my glass window of perfection. I was fallible, and my alter self revolted.

I first started jogging excessively. Then the jogging wasn't enough, so I altered my diet. Every time I looked in the mirror, I saw lumps everywhere. I was drastically losing weight, but the imperfections remained.

I considered the sugar content in the alcohol, but without alcohol, he wouldn't see me. I started smoking cigarettes. The tobacco heightened my metabolism and kept me thin while I continued to drink. I would get up in the morning and jog off the sugars that sat dormant over night while I was sleeping and inactive.

It wasn't enough. It was never enough.

The mirror was God—an idol—and I bowed to its reflection, and met its every command. I had a new obsession and it consumed me. I started controlling my diet with diuretics at the end of each day. This continued for a couple of years.

I was engrossed in obtaining the perfect me, which equaled perfect love. Because perfect love equaled being seen.

I saw nothing but a perfectly painted picture of forever, and as a result, I missed his declining interest in me.

The obsession and control to keep my body perfect was destructive, and it wasn't long before I became extremely sick. My insides were in constant, excruciating pain. Exhaustion ruled, and depression grew. My body screamed for help, and I was afraid to let its failures show. In an obscure way to be seen, I went to great lengths to keep myself hidden.

I was a mess. By the third year, Tom broke up with me. Again, I pleaded with every desperate attempt to amend any failures that caused the breakup, but he was done. Anything that was left of me died that day.

Isolated and alone, stranded on the very island I created, I contemplated suicide. I reached out to my mom. She had just finished her rehab and was healthy and working at a new job. We hadn't seen each other for some time, and there was much mending needed between us. I asked her to come to me.

It was Christmas, and the company where I was employed was having a party, so she took some time off and drove a few hours just to see me. I prepared for hope. Throwing all I had left into expectation.

She showed up in a beautiful black velvet dress, and we sat on a nearby bench. I wanted to share with her, tell her everything. But because my mom appeared so frail, I was afraid to burden her. I sat there next to her. She looked contented. Christmas music played in the background.

She left that weekend, and we never discussed any of the problems making me feel more desperate than before.

My health declined steadily from keeping it all inside and hidden, and the only coping mechanism I knew was to drink it away. I met more people at the dance clubs, so I went back to the bars. I was barely out of the breakup with Tom, still grieving and very much in love with him, when I met someone else.

*Isaac was the most attentive human being I had ever met. The *open-doors-for-you* kind of man. He wouldn't allow me to pay for anything, and made sure I was taken care of at all costs. With him, there was never any hesitation. I felt secure.

While we were dating, my doctor diagnosed me with anorexia and endometriosis. He scheduled me for my first endometrial surgery. I had a high probability of having no children, and this grieved me.

Isaac showed up, took me in, and cared for me. I don't know if it was because I was still in love with someone else, or if the deeper connection just wasn't there with Isaac; whichever it was, I said yes to a relationship with him and moved into his house almost right away.

At the time, I was working at an OBGYN office, and began having unique symptoms. I wondered if it was post-surgery complications. Cramps and nausea came often. I brought my symptoms to the head nurse, and she asked me to take a pregnancy test.

She met me in the back room with tears of joy in her eyes. "You're pregnant." She was elated, and I was in shock. So many things went through my mind. I never wanted to have children—was told I couldn't have children. Would Isaac accept me as a mother of his child? Twenty-four years old and my life was on the line. I would have to quit so many things, and I did not know if I was capable.

I held onto the news alone for several days, nervous and unsure what the future might hold, while I gathered the strength to tell him.

We were driving down the road when I suddenly blurted out, "I'm pregnant."

Isaac stopped the car. Trying to hide a smile, he said, "Whatever you choose to do, I support you."

For the first time in an exceedingly long time, I felt seen. "I want to keep the baby."

I stopped drinking and started living free from chemical dependency. This allowed pieces of my old self to re-emerge. Family became the new obsession. The vision turned from living together and romantic adventures, to wanting the white picket fence, marriage, and a family full of traditions.

If I envisioned it, Isaac provided. We had everything we needed financially. Every piece of furniture, the home, the new car, food, and clothing. I did not care that I could not feel intimate with him because that had actively caused me pain in the past. Our connection was an endearing friendship. We had a beautiful child together, I loved him as family.

When our daughter turned one, I became increasingly discontented. My soul was starved for family, and none of the material things our girl's father provided could feed it. I was unsatisfied with solely dating the father of my daughter, and believed marriage was the solution.

I started pressing him for an engagement. Isaac was not ready, and this caused much friction in our friendship.

Unable to bear the possibility of rejection, I turned my back on him and began planning a wedding anyway. All that mattered was this marriage, and it was contingent on the engagement, and Isaac was the one who had to ask. I needed him to ask; asking was significant. Asking meant he wanted me.

It was a renaissance dream event, every detail planned—without the engagement. My longing ran deep, and I was invested more in the idea than I was in the father of my child.

One day we were shopping downtown, and I started in on the engagement, obsessively begging him and describing the ring I wanted. Isaac parked the car, got out, and slammed the door. I stayed in the passenger side, waiting for him to cool off. After some time, he came back, opened the door, and threw a little black box on my lap. It was the engagement ring. He had thrown it at me in frustration, but I had set myself up for it. It was an engagement ring.

It wasn't long before we broke up.

I destroyed the dream and was disgusted with myself again. I was incapable of relationships and quickly started to doubt myself as a mother. It was difficult to come to terms with it all, however, with me carrying the burden of the breakup, I found it much easier to remain friends and co-parent.

Me being the mother of his child, he let my vision for marriage dissolve and still cared for me and supported me.

I took full advantage of his care for me, despite our breakup. Co-parenting gave me too much time alone. When Isaac had our daughter, my loneliness became tangible, and so I went back to the place where I felt most seen—the bar.

I lived a dual life. A mother during the week, overcompensating with attentiveness and good intentions, filling my daughter up emotionally so that I could move through the weekend without guilt. And a weekend partier, living as the center of attention. Like a drug, the night life filled the void and pain of feeling unwanted and unseen. I thrived off it so much that it bled over into the week, and my motherhood took second place.

The nightlife was my stage, and the audience loved me. My new personality emerged as one that wore revealing costumes and performed seductive dance moves. I wasn't a mother or a girlfriend. I wasn't pretending to be someone else. And I never had to retreat to my safe space. I was the life of the party, trying to outdo myself with every passing week.

There was one long back road in the area that connected two small towns. On either side of the road there were about six local bars, and each had its own unique style. A few were known for their regular patrons, the others for their excessive drinkingA couple of the establishments boasted late night, club-style dancing.

Hopping from one bar to the next, I often stayed after hours and got to know everyone. Bartenders became friends, and drinks were free. Gathering groups of girls with me, the security would let us walk past the long lines of people and usher us through the entrance. Like modern day influencers, we would bring the place to life.

I favored one bar because I knew the owner. He had just hired a new DJ named *Dan. The bar wasn't large, but it was long, with the alcohol at the front and the dance floor at the very back. It was difficult in its crowded space to move from one end to the other—except this night.

Standing at the bar—the music loud, the smell of perfume and sweat lingering in my nose, excitement rising—I turned toward the dance floor with a drink in my hand. The crowd appeared to part just for me, giving me a glimpse of the DJ.

When I saw him, every unhealthy part of me leapt with desire, and nothing else mattered. I pursued him immediately, walking straight up to the booth. Introducing myself like a business card with credentials—

who I knew, and who I was *because* of who I knew. He didn't even look at me when he answered me flatly with a "Hey."

I wasn't used to the lack of attention, let alone his unwillingness to even turn toward me. Instead of offense, it catapulted me into a place of further desire. If a man did not want me and was not taking advantage of an opportunity to go home with me, he must be safe and genuine!

Nothing else mattered to me but having him. I showed up every chance I got, relentlessly pursuing him until he said yes to a date. We went on several, and each time I morphed into whatever he wanted. I was enamored by his fast-paced life.

Dan introduced me to the world of underground festivals. The perceived freedom and genuineness the people projected captivated me. The language, music, style, and the way they belonged to each other through one simple understanding.

Their community encompassed all things concerning peace, love, unity, and utmost respect. It was like the words of the Bible without binding by religious law. It was belonging.

My relationship with the Dan was fluid. We never labeled it. In the world in which he lived, there were no labels. I never asked questions, just moved with it all.

He invited me to a party. Moving through the room, there were fire dancers, bubbles, and sequins for days. You would see small groups laughing and dancing, or find couples making out on the couch.

These parties had limited alcohol, but plenty of water, citrus juice, and trays filled with a selection of marijuana and pills. Everyone had such inclusivity and respect for life that nothing ever felt like a threat to me.

That night, Dan brought me into his room and sat me down on his bed. He asked me if I wanted to try an ecstasy pill. Quickly saying no, I explained I would never do drugs, because I never wanted to feel like I was outside of myself. Drugs would give the devil access to my life. But the truth was, he already had a backstage pass to my soul.

Dan explained the history behind the drug, how it affected you in ways allowing you to still be in control, but with an intensity that stimulated parts of your brain that already existed. He offered me half a pill and offered to stay with me the whole night. He ensured my safety because it was not like other drugs.

Within thirty minutes, it hit me. I took one sudden deep breath and my senses came alive. Dan escorted me through little journeys: a feather, a plush pillow, water, and then a kiss. My body was abuzz with every touch, my entire being floating with ecstasy. When he kissed me, I vibrated with pleasure. This kind of pleasure was unmatched. With just a single touch, my body awakened from its slumber. I never wanted it to stop. I asked him for more and continued to want more for months.

Dan came to me with news that he was moving to a larger metropolitan area in California. I could not live without him or the drug. He invited me to move with him. I wanted to go, but was ashamed at the thought of leaving my daughter behind. Choosing his life over hers would have certainly ended mine, so I decided to take her with me.

My family and my daughter's father were all completely unaware of my drug use. No one was happy with me leaving, but nobody had reason to stop me. With a plan in place for me to have her during the week and her father picking her up on the weekends, I packed and moved with Dan—the one I couldn't live without.

In a whirlwind of moments, I encountered nightlife on a larger scale. There is this force that happens after hours in the city. It pushes you to keep going until the sun rises, but there is always dread if you meet the sunrise. There were Cinderella moments, escaping into the night and pushing myself to the next level, using more drugs until the clock struck sunrise, then racing home and trying to sleep with my body and mind buzzing.

I couldn't function throughout the week when coming off ecstasy. Overwhelmed with anxiety and depression, my senses were in a constant state of chaos. Dan and I began fighting a lot, our relationship toxic. We argued anywhere and everywhere. I blamed it on coming down off the drug.

I cut pills in half to create a sort of supplement, just to get by. I continued to do this until I reached a point where the drug would have no effect on me, so I had to use more. I was taking two to three ecstasy pills during my workday and sometimes one at night, and by the weekend, I needed more just to feel anything.

There was one night when an underground event was taking place. They used an old hotel, the rooms filled with different aesthetics. Moving from room to room was an adventure, something new to try.

I did not want to miss out on anything, and continued to consume anything and everything in each room until it was time to go home. We almost always had to plan on staying out all night and finding a ride home, or leaving early and taking the last subway ride home. This night, Dan and I rode the subway home.

I had sampled too many pills and was in some strange, altered state, in and out of consciousness, with flashes of lucid thoughts and memories. When I was lucid, I could see that I was losing time, frightening me.

We were on the subway still, and every time my mind became conscious of what was right in front of me, I saw a different scene. The first time my mind became aware, the subway appeared empty, dark and desolate, yet lights bright and flashing. I saw a lone man sitting across the aisle, staring at me with intent. I stared back. The longer I looked at him, the more his face morphed into some demonic presence with a predatory smile. I felt trapped, and it scared me. I leaned into Dan, and my mind left again.

The next time I became lucid, there were more people. They were laughing at me, pointing, and mocking me. I left again, until once again I was lucid. This time I saw the souls of everyone. Their eyes were dark and mocking. They brought death and destruction. They were demons in the guise of humans. Extremely paranoid of what was I doing in the unconscious state, I felt like was I losing control of myself, my mind never completely returning to reality.

The last time I was lucid, I was in our apartment. We were in Dan's room having sex. Even though we had an intimate relationship, this was different. I was unaware of how I got there, and was terrified.

I was making choices in an altered state of mind, and Dan was making choices for me as if I were clear with my intent. I felt assaulted by the unconscious mind. I wanted to throw up. I wanted to scream and run. Everything was out of control, and I did not want Dan to know I was losing it.

For the first time in years—and right in the middle of having sex—I cried out to God in prayer, internally pleading with him to bring me back to sanity, while demanding to know if He existed. I then bartered with Him: "God, I would forever be indebted to you if I wake up from this… I will not do drugs again." That was the last memory I had before waking up a day later with a clear, sound mind.

I tried several times to quit using ecstasy, but it was too difficult. I cut back once again, taking only half of what I had before. But continuing to use drugs on a lesser scale allowed shame in, nullifying my promise to God. I was convinced that he was ashamed of me too.

Ecstasy affects serotonin and dopamine in the brain. When combined with extensive use of alcohol and marijuana, it was causing severe cognitive issues with my mood, memory, and anxiety. These issues spilled over and into my relationship, my job, and my motherhood.[2]

My mom and the father of my child both saw me rapidly declining and conspired to pull my daughter from my life. For her safety, but also in hope it would be enough for me to change my life. Taking my daughter from me was a symbol of all the lies in my life, feeding shame's vortex and catapulting me further into a destructive state.

Dan and I would get in such needless, volatile arguments, and I ended up in dangerous situations—like jumping out of a moving car in the middle of the road. I was in a destructive downward spiral.

I had two jobs, both in retail. At one job, I was stealing bags of clothes and concocting ways to get all the employees on board with me. The other job was more rigid in following procedures, but the manager was always kind to me and took me under her wing. Looking back, I was a horrible employee, always tired and moody, affecting my ability to show up and how I treated customers.

I needed both jobs to get by, and living paycheck to paycheck made it very difficult to save money to move toward regaining custody of my daughter. I was fired from one job, causing a chain of events that spiraled me into severe depression. Without the job, I could not pay for my car, and it was repossessed. I had no way home, and no way to my other job.

Within the week, the manager at my second job pulled me into a meeting. I broke down in front of my manager, telling her everything. Ready to be let go and very ready to tell someone the truth, I laid it all out at the table. Sobbing uncontrollably, we sat in that moment for what felt like an eternity, when she finally said, "Let's get you help and get you back to your daughter. It is not too late to turn your life around. God loves you too much for me to let you leave like this."

She had every reason as a manager to fire me, but she kept me working. Her faithful heart saw me through the eyes of God, and that moment was the catalyst toward a shift in my life, a shift toward truth.

5

THE LIE: IT DOESN'T MATTER - PART 1

*"In my distress I cried out to you, the delivering God, and from
your temple-throne you heard my troubled cry, and my sobs
went right into your heart." Psalm 18:6*

THE PLAY WAS OVER, THE CURTAIN drawn, the lights out. The seats were empty, and everyone had gone home. My time in the spotlight was over. A dark force moved in on me, like a puppet master taking control. Giving way to it because nothing else mattered.

Dan and broke up, and I went back to my hometown. Sleeping on floors and couches, I was homeless and suffering from addiction to alcohol and drugs with no money to fuel it. I was desperate.

The first time begging for money at a local gas station was disgusting, but desperation to fuel the addiction superseded my discomfort. Throwing on a smile and a bold lie, I told each person I had run out of gas.

I didn't appear homeless. Instead, I was a young, scantily dressed woman who needed help, and people gave generously. I invested the funds in more pills and sold them at the local bars, paying the puppet master.

It was difficult to find ecstasy in the rural area in which I lived, so I began attending house parties again. From experience, I remembered the colorful trays filled with every drug desired, and these were the places I found to be more profitable for my addiction.

I ended up at a house party of a family member. In the back room, there was a full-body mirror laying on the bed. Several people surrounded it, bent over and snorting a white substance up their nose.

In all my experiences, this was my first exposure to cocaine. One woman who knew me well, jumped up and ran at me, trying her best to convince me that whatever was in the room was not for me. She tried to push me back outside the bedroom door, while my mind raced with a million thoughts. Knowing that this drug was more accessible than the struggles I faced to maintain my ecstasy addiction, I convinced her right back.

After all, I in my early twenties, certainly old enough to make my own choices. Anyway, it was just for this evening and only to party. Nobody could stop me from it, and I argued that if I didn't do it in the safety of a room with people I knew, I would go elsewhere. She backed off, and I walked over and snorted my first line of cocaine.

Like a landslide, cocaine carried me with it. Day after day, night after night, I used drugs. I was the life of the party and, because of that, I wanted more. I quickly bypassed the middleman, gaining access to the drug directly from the seller and turning a profit to support my habit.

I was so good at it; I became the connection. Top seller of all drugs: cocaine, marijuana, and a plethora of additional pills. I stepped outside the bar scene and began following music festivals, gained backstage access, and sold to prominent people in the music industry.

There was a need to show my life was progressing positively so I could have visitation with my daughter. The money from selling drugs and the people I met helped me obtain a rental apartment and a part-time job. Finally, I had my daughter two to three days a week.

On the days she stayed with me, I stopped using drugs and alcohol. I was protecting her, but it ultimately did more damage. During the two days she came, I was coming off drugs, moody, and sleeping more than half the day away.

Each week, on Sunday, my uncle showed up and asked me to go to church. Drug sick, I would answer the door and say no. Then he'd take my daughter to church, which gave me time to wake up so I could spend some quality time with her before her father came to pick her up.

On visitation days, I lived the life of being a good mom, pretending to be sober. But I was in so much pain from withdrawal, that when my daughter left for her father's, I would double down on the drugs. My life was full of shame. Shame told me my life did not matter and my child was better off without me.

After about a year, I took a turn for the worse, and was arrested several times for being drunk and disorderly and driving while intoxicated. But nothing was stopping me, not even the fact that my body was failing, and death was knocking at the door.

Weighing 80 pounds, I was emaciated and pale. The party life faded out, and I began using alone, getting high every day in my apartment. I could not afford my addiction, and would make desperate attempts at getting high by using a safety pen to dig out the residue in the cracks of the table, or by turning my pockets inside out just to get any powder that had spilled over. I snorted the residue of powder and everything with it. I invited dealers into my home to do business just for a trade, putting myself in extremely dangerous and illegal situations with large amounts of cocaine in my house.

The use of drugs caused paranoia, and I heard voices and saw demons regularly. Voices of shame and despair seeped through the ceiling cracks, and I was convinced people were watching me from the apartment above through tiny cameras lowered down through the fan lights. Continuous whispers of disgust constantly came to me in the night. I once heard demons laughing and mocking me through my living room window.

I lost all hope and sense of reality, until one day when I had my daughter for a visit. I usually had all the doors shut in the studio so she would be safe in the room while I slept. Somehow the front part of the door to the entryway came open and she was digging around in my shoes. I woke up frantically looking for her and found her holding a small baggy of cocaine. Shaking it in between her tiny little fingers, she extended it to me as a gift with an innocent grin. I grabbed the bag and threw it away as if it were a venomous snake, then I scooped my daughter up into my arms.

I wept for her life and gave thanks to God, repenting every single choice leading me to that moment there with my daughter. I called on Jesus by name, begging him for forgiveness. And with every repenting statement, demons fled, screaming and screeching on their way out. I lay there with my daughter, holding her, sobbing and exhausted from the battle.

After nearly two years of drugs, I was done, with nowhere to go and no resources to turn to. Having worked in the mental field, I was concerned if I got help I'd be committed and lose access to my daughter. So, remaining silent, isolating myself in the apartment, I went through withdrawal alone. Dope sick, the nights were the worse. It was nothing I had experienced before, and it wasn't just a physical withdrawal, but a spiritual battle over my mind.

The body aches were excruciating, as if someone were taking a bat to my bones. My stomach twisted as if a searing hot knife was blading through, causing me to protrude bodily functions from every which way. Sweating profusely yet feeling cold, with my head throbbing all hours, I wanted out.

The spiritual battle over my mind seemed like a journey through a perilous storm with heavy a snow blizzard freezing me to the point of death. I had hypothermia of life. Hypothermia creates a weak pulse, loss of consciousness, confusion, and often death. And that was right where I was—near death. The voices warred with thoughts, trying to release me of the pain with only one more use of the drug.

Screaming out for Jesus to release me, a sudden warmth came over me. My temperature rose, thawing me from the inside out. Jesus met me there, His arms swooping me into a comforting embrace. All fear left. He was safe, and so I just closed my eyes and slept.

Needing family, I called my dad. He lived in Hawaii at the time, and I asked him to come home. My dad didn't know what was going on in my life, aside from the occasional call from jail. When he showed up, shame flooded me in indescribable ways. He was a man of God, respected by many in the church, and his very appearance was significant to my failure as a daughter of a pastor and, even more, as a daughter.

He sat directly across from me at a local coffee shop. I told him I wanted to talk to him about something very important, but did not want to hear any "God stuff" or be pastored by him. I just wanted my dad. I told him I was an addict and needed help.

I ignored his response, explaining how I got there and giving a barrage of excuses why I was an addict. Suddenly stopping, we sat there in awkward silence for what seemed like forever.

Offended, I broke the silence by asking why he wasn't responding. He said, "God is in me, and if you do not want to hear *God stuff*, then I have nothing to say." My dad held me tight that day and continued to support me, this moment had an everlasting impact on my life and kindled a curiosity toward God.

I told my family members the truth, exposing myself to them one by one. The accountability in the struggle with addiction gave me strength to persevere and released me from the lies that were bound by addiction.

One afternoon while driving, a memory flashed through my thoughts—my uncle coming by the house each week while in the middle of my addiction, asking me to go to church. I watched myself turn him down each week. My heart pulled toward family as the memory of seeing each of their attempts to help me through the years drew me back. Tears streaked my face; I looked up to find myself in the parking lot of a church I had attended as a child. I walked inside.

For weeks following, I would attend if their doors were open. I was resistant to the message and spoke to no one. Standing in the back completely shut down, trying to remain invisible to the world, something deep inside urged me to grab a Bible. I stole one from the back, slipped it into my jacket, and went home. In the same space I used drugs and gave up my body for sex, where I met with dealers and heard from demons, I began reading my Bible and praying. For three months I read, from the time I woke until I went to sleep.

When I was young, the Bible was proclaimed as law over my life. But this time, when reading through the gospel, I could enter the stories within the scripture, taking each verse and applying it as a set boundary to keep me out of addiction.

I landed a new job at a child psychiatric office as a manager. This job activated hidden pieces of me, and I started to feel worthy of something good.

The job was within walking distance of a dive bar where I used to party. Walking home one St. Patrick's Day, people were out everywhere, laughing and singing. It had been so long since I laughed like that. Withdrawal was hard, but then I met loneliness.

Not only was I leaving drugs, but also the lifestyle built over the years: loyal friendships, deep connections, my entire social life. My entire identity as a young adult was wrapped around it all. There was no thing or label I could hide behind. Naked and vulnerable. Stranded in foreign space. No idea who I was.

The laughter jarred a part of my old self awake, the self that needed to be surrounded again. The street was buzzing with people and I wanted to be a part of it. I reached into my purse and found six dollars. Enough for two beers and then I would go home. I turned back around and headed to the bar.

Unbeknownst to me, a man, *Jay, spotted me from a distance. He watched me cross the street and followed me into the bar. I took a seat at the bar and ordered one beer. He sat near me and ordered a drink. By the time I ordered my second beer, he had found his way to the stool next to me and into conversation.

We laughed and joked as if we had known each other for years. It felt good to laugh again. He was kind and hilarious. Jay was also a father; this represented all things supportive and safe. Right away, he told me he missed his kids, and he was in a fight to get them back. Their mother had kidnapped them, and his story was heartfelt and desperate. What a beautiful man to want a family, but it had been taken from him. We closed the place down, and I went home.

I considered myself a success story going home after only two beers and meeting a new friend. There was self-control, and this was health. Jay invited me out several times over the next month. He introduced me to new music, took me on actual dates, and introduced me to friends. I would drink only a beer and maintain self-control every time. And he would walk me home.

While we were dating, I ran into an old friend who was a dealer. He pulled me aside and offered me a "bump" of cocaine. I turned it down, but struggled the rest of the night with wanting to use. The struggle escalated into shots of hard alcohol, and by the end of the night, I was drunk.

Jay became increasingly jealous and protective as the night went on, and we ended up in a heated argument. I went home that night carrying the full weight of responsibility for the argument. Afraid of my new vulnerable state of mind, as well as the potential of poor choices destroying my relationship, I surrendered myself to him.

Giving complete admittance to who I spoke to, how much I drank, my schedule, and my immediate whereabouts. I was losing my independence at a rapid rate, but having had independence before proved to put me in places that were lethal to my life, and so I allowed him to regulate every aspect of my life.

On Easter Sunday, my daughter was with her father, and the rest of my family had plans. Jay was a chef and was called into work for the day, and so I read the Bible for most of the morning. But again, the loneliness was too much to bear. Coupled with the pressure of losing my independence, it all became too much for me. I shut the Bible and left for the bar.

When I entered the room, it was dark and empty. The smell of musty, spilled beer raised my senses as I took my seat at the end of the bar and ordered a beer. It was resurrection day, and I had chosen to sit in ruin.

After a while, I heard the door open and a man in a long black trench coat walked in. The hood hid his face, but I felt his presence—the puppet master was back. A scene played out as the bartender turned his back to me, as if masking himself from something he didn't want to see. Without one word, the man in the trench coat came over and promptly laid out a line of cocaine on the bar right in front of me.

Defeated and under the control of the puppet master, I bent over and started snorting the line.

Halfway through, a penetrating voice yelled,

"Stop!"

It was God. I shuddered with conviction.

"I have been calling for you, but you haven't heard me—the parties are too loud. I have put my arms around you, and you do not feel me—sex has become your comfort. I have been protecting you, but you go around me—the drugs have numbed you. Turn away from this life and listen to me. I have something special planned for you. Let us go."

Still hunched over and crippled helpless, a single tear ran down my cheek. Somehow, I found courage through the voice of God. I looked up to face my demon, but he was gone. I violently dragged my hand through the half line of cocaine, shook it off to the floor, and ran out.

Easter Sunday, the day of resurrection, I was saved.

Around 2003, when I was 29 years old, my daughter was living with me, and we attended church regularly; I focused on my relationship with Jay.

We moved in together while he was going through his divorce process. This was very stressful, and he hoped to have custody of his two boys. When he yelled sharply at me or my daughter, my compassion for his situation superseded the pain of our arguments, and so I catered to whatever provided peace in our home.

When I found out I was pregnant, the news changed Jay's behavior tremendously. He became more protective of me, claiming me as a possession since the seed I carried contained his DNA. However, his need to see his boys grew more desperate, and our home became a minefield of explosives. One wrong move or word could set him off.

With God in my life, desire for family was stronger than ever, but Jay wanted to go out with his friends and drink. His partying created an unstable foundation for me. We argued half the week. I knew he missed his boys, and the tension of his divorce was too much for one person to go through. Each time I allowed him to act in that way, and with every argument I excused, I gave up a piece of myself. I didn't trust the situation or how to live in it, and so I succumbed to his will.

At four months into pregnancy, it was Jay's birthday. We were sleeping soundly, when I woke to wet sheets. I reached down and felt between my legs. Blood. I yanked back the sheets. There was blood everywhere, and I ran into the bathroom and sat on the toilet, sobbing with pain and fear. He stood in the bathroom doorway, both asking if I needed help and sharing his disappointment this was happening on his birthday.

I was in shock and needed help, but he was so disconnected. I felt bad for him, frantically wondering what I could do to ease his own discomfort above my own. Thinking maybe he was afraid, I sent him to go get my mom, who lived only down the road.

Sitting in that bathroom alone, I screamed out apologies to God for whatever I had done that would be punishable by the death of my child. The bleeding worsened, then there was a sharp cramping pain with pressure. I innately reached down just as a large mass fell into my hands. Pulling my hands up close to my chest, blood dripping everywhere, it took me a moment to realize I was holding my baby.

Looking down at a little pink human in my hand, all the hurts and pains of my life added up to this one moment, and a tidal wave of injustice rose from deep within my soul and came screaming out in a deep wail, piercing the silence.

I went to the space in my mind, the dissociative space. I had not been there in so many years, but there it was, waiting for me, holding me close. I stayed there until my mom showed up and cared for me.

For months, I punished myself for the miscarriage, blaming myself for the drug use, and blaming myself for not being a good mother to the daughter I did have. I was convinced this was a punishment from God for being promiscuous.

Turning toward what I knew of redemption, if I could just be a good Christian, God would bless me. I poured myself into scripture to become a good woman of good works. Made many promises to God. Submitted to Jay and quickly became pregnant again.

Becoming pregnant so soon after the miscarriage, my emotions were at an all-time high. Our finances were depleted, and there was the continued battle for his boys. It was too stressful at home, walking on eggshells to keep things peaceful, and going into overdrive to keep the place nice and tidy. I strived to have meals ready by the time Jay came home from work. But no matter what I did, he would always find something he hated, and I would always rationalize every complaint.

Often, Jay would come home late and drunk. Many nights I knew he was talking to or hanging out with female friends. I hated it and often wondered if he was cheating. Broaching anything like that would end up in an argument, and I would sob myself to sleep.

One evening, Jay came home and had obviously been drinking. He started in on me about how there were more pictures of my daughter than his boys on the walls. Angry they were mostly of my family, he pulled down the pictures, yelling at me. I begged him to stop, and then he took a picture of my daughter and threw it to the ground, shattering glass everywhere.

Screaming only enraged him further, and he lunged at me, his face red and his eyes dark. I ran toward the door, and he leaped around me, blocking the exit, telling me I would never leave.

In this moment, I became defensive, because it was not about me anymore. We had a child to think about. I pushed him with all my strength. He stood firm, giving me more incentive. In one last effort, I pushed again. This time he pulled back, gained his footing. Like a slingshot, he lunged, slugging me in my pregnant belly.

A searing pain flashed across my body as I tumbled back and rolled into a fetal position, remaining like that until he left the room. I got up on all fours, scurried across the floor to the open door, and ran out into the street.

Barefoot. Wearing only a long t-shirt and underwear. Freezing cold and pouring down rain. I held my belly tight and ran as fast as I could down the road until I reached my mother's apartment complex two miles away.

I was sopping wet, freezing. She had barely buzzed me in, when Jay showed up screaming into the intercom, telling her that he had ownership over me now. He made several threats toward her, and then it went silent.

I laid on her couch for several hours before deciding to go back. Mom wanted to keep me there, but I went anyway.

I gasped when I saw the shattered, broken mess. Jay had broken and ripped every photo on the wall. Every scrap was a representation of my heart, and I bent over and picked up a ripped picture of my family. I made my way through the room, clutching the photo to my chest. Jay was passed out on the bed. I spent the rest of the evening cleaning up the mess, restoring a semblance of normalcy.

When we woke up in the morning, he turned to me with a huge smile, pulling me in and holding me tight. I snuggled in and kissed him. Maybe he didn't remember, maybe it was just a one-time incident and none of it mattered except for the moment we were sharing.

By the end of the year, we were engaged. It was nothing I expected. The simplicity of the engagement after years of hunger for a family allowed me to say yes, and not too long after the engagement that we were walking down the aisle.

6

THE LIE: IT DOESN'T MATTER - PART 2

WE MARRIED IN 2004. I WAS NEARLY eight months pregnant, squeezed into a whimsical wedding dress, and surrounded by family at a beautiful location overlooking the ocean.

When it was nearing time to give birth, Jay made it very clear that nobody would be allowed in the room except him. Too nervous to disagree with him, but also very nervous that my family, who had been at the birth of every grandchild, would miss out, I kept the peace. That is, until the day of delivery, when most of my family showed up and slipped into the delivery room. Jay was obviously upset, but I was in the safety of family surrounding me, and he did nothing.

It was a long, difficult labor. Our baby girl became stuck, and they had to use forceps to pull her out. By the time she was birthed, she wasn't breathing. It all happened so fast, leaving me traumatized and exhausted. She cried a lot in the first month, so I brought her in for a check-up. They found she had a broken clavicle from the hard birth. It was difficult, but a miracle, and to me signified God's blessing.

Both my daughters were at my side, finally bringing a sense of family, a sense of peace and happiness that entered the home.

Our daughter was not even a year old when we received a phone call from his ex-wife's family. She had died tragically in a car accident. Once we received this call, there were a series of events, legal actions, and emotional decisions that brought the boys home with us. Our immediate, newly blended family of six consisted of a new baby, two emotionally traumatized boys, and my oldest daughter, who was six years old.

The ex-wife's family consistently fought for the boys. It all was so confusing to me. She was the one who "kidnapped" the kids, and his obvious attempts were because he wanted them back in his life. Why were the grandparents so adamant about it all? I stood by Jay and believed all that he told me.

During the court process, the drug task force was called on Jay for an old warrant on drug charges. He was arrested and put into jail, leaving me with four children under the age of six, no job or finances to pay the bills, and a very sick baby. I was so scared that they were going to come take the children in his absence, I gathered all the money I could and hid in a dive motel, waiting to hear from the judge.

It was all too much for me. I was doubting my marriage when I received an incredibly well-written letter from Jay. He apologized for his past actions and promised me safety and the utmost protection when he got out. My doubt relieved, I reached out to family and pushed through.

Following Jay's release from jail, things were fantastic—for a while. Then he began drinking and going out again. One night he came home so late I had locked the door. This enraged him—he was yelling and banging on the door, trying to make his way in. Frightened, I backed myself up against the headboard, pulled my knees to my chest, and stayed there, awake, until he fell asleep outside the door. In the morning, everything went back to normal. It always did.

There was a time Jay requested a babysitter and asked me to come out with him. I was so excited and put a lot into getting ready. Jay had a preferred style; he loved a hippie woman. He loved dreadlocks, flowy clothes, patchouli oil, and an unshaved body. I would do anything in exchange for his kindness, and if that meant having hair on my legs or armpits, I honored it.

This night, I shaved and dressed up just for him. I lifted my arms and twirled around, expecting approval. Instead, he screamed at me with disgust. I had not asked his permission to shave, and he was angry. I defended myself this time, and that came at a cost.

We tussled and argued for a bit, but when his eyes showed rage and his voice sharp, it frightened me, and I ran into the bathroom for safety. Lying there on the cold tile floor, I embraced the rusty, cracked foot of the old bathtub, anchoring myself for the storm.

Sitting there in the calm, alert for the sounds of his feet approaching, I watched the dust settle in the bathroom. As the motes swirled, they caught the sunbeams streaming through the bathroom window, creating a cascading stream of glitter. I stared into the safety of the glistening beam and prayed.

This moment of peace was broken by a rumble in the distance. Hysteria. When Jay allowed hysteria in, there was no turning back, and verbal and physical violence always followed. I fled to the safe space in my mind, but I was abruptly pulled back out when Jay came bursting into the bathroom and twisted his fists in my hair.

Grabbing me by a handful of dreadlocks, he dragged me out and across the bedroom floor to the closet, where he shoved me inside and slammed the door. What was happening to me?

The darkness of the closet wrapped around me with the heaviness of both comfort and burden. A single shaft of light peeked through the crack at the bottom of the door, and once again I stared into the safety of the beautiful glistening sunbeam and prayed.

I decided to see a therapist, hopeful we would find resolution as a family. But each visit became a manipulative stage play throwing responsibility onto to me. Jay insisted that I had "lost it" or I was "crazy," and encouraged the therapist I needed further help. Believing everything he was saying, I became depressed and anxious. I exhibited obvious signs of obsessive-compulsive disorder, and walked away from every therapy session crushed.

It wasn't easy caring for four children under six, but I was unwavering in my love for them all, and more determined than ever to become a better wife and mother. I adopted the two boys. An overwhelming love swooped in and took over my heart. My love for the kids was vast, one that resides in the depths of my heart today.

Around 2016, we moved near my dad on the island of Oahu. Being near my dad and his wife created a safe environment, and gave me hope. I went over first with the two girls and bought a car and found a rental. Jay followed later with the two boys and was immediately hired on a new job. I found a local church to attend; the kids went to school. It was beautiful time for us as a family.

My oldest daughter was enamored with the love of community, she began to read the Bible every morning before school. She prayed for me, asking God every morning for me to see Him in the way she did. Watching my daughter gave me so much hope, I turned to God and restored my relationship with him. As my faith grew, so did my children's. It was then my daughter was baptized.

My relationship with God gave me instant community in the church, becoming friends with the pastor's wife and attending women's ministry. The pastor's wife was the very first person of many that would turn to me and tell me I was going to be a woman of great faith, leading many to Christ.

When Jay and I met, he was Mormon. He left Mormonism for Christianity. He loved God and believed in Him, but was not as involved as I was. I wanted very much for my husband to feel the love of God like the kids and I did. He went to church when he could and praised God in worship, but it seemed with every step of confidence that I took toward the Lord's voice, Jay would take a step back and away from me.

He was working seventeen-hour shifts and meeting his own friends on the other side of the island, while I was caring for the kids on my own. I had little to no social life outside the church. When he came home, there was so much disconnect between us. The yelling started again.

He was changing, his eyes dark, and his heart hardened. There were times when emergencies came up. He would brush them off as minor incidents that had the potential to get in the way of his hours at work. One night I woke in the middle of the night in a lot of pain, but was too nervous to wake him. I slid off the side of the bed and crawled across the floor.

The pain ultimately worsened, and I had no choice but to wake him. He was annoyed when I asked him to take me to the hospital, and told me he had to be work in just a few hours. He rolled over and went back to sleep while I crawled toward the door with a phone in my hand, calling my dad's house for a ride. I passed several kidney stones that night.

One time, our daughter swallowed a toy that got lodged in her chest. She was choking and vomiting bile. With our only vehicle with Jay at work, I called the ambulance. Me (and all my children) rushed to the emergency room. Jay called from work and asked if he really needed to be there, since everything seemed to be taken care of. He never showed up. From that night, my parents saw a need in our marriage and encouraged Jay with wisdom.

On Jay's days off, he went surfing. Even though it took away from intimacy or connection with me and the kids, we gave him space to do it. If he didn't have an outlet on his days off, he would be restless, and restlessness was an ingredient to annoyance, which led to anger.

His anger was getting worse. We had a little dog sometimes barked and whined, setting Jay off. She was barking insistently one afternoon, so I ran outside to quiet her down. I found Jay holding her up by the neck beating her. I screamed. He dropped her, then blamed me for the noise. I apologized for not having gotten there sooner.

Periodically, Jay would come home and have fun plans for the family. He would take me on dates, bringing home gifts and beautiful, endearing letters. When he was affectionate and playful with me and the kids, we created short memories, times so precious to us. We held them up higher than the painful ones. During one period of peace, he came home with news that we would be moving to another island—the island of Kauai.

I obliged, knowing there was no other way but his. But inside I was deeply afraid of becoming isolated, moving even further away from our church community, family, and friends.

After moving to the new island in 2008, Jay was just like when we first met, full of fun and laughter. He introduced me to his coworkers; we would all go out and have family time on the beach. People came over often, and we built a beautiful community of friendships.

The kids attended a local school where they became a part of the Hawaiian culture, and I found a church to attend on Sundays. Although Jay attended church on Sunday, he grew more interested in another religion—Ethiopian Orthodox. In the time that we had been together—over five years—Jay had taken three different religious beliefs and started to create something of his own. There was a firm system put into place where I had to be a submissive wife: ask before you do, and honor the husband at all costs. This shifted Jay into old patterns once again.

The drugs returned. I would often find glass pipes lying around. He was drinking heavily again, and the anger was now directed toward the children. It got so bad, he was unable to control himself.

When my friends and any family, in-laws included, visited, they would question his behavior. His reaction was to project their intent onto me, which would ultimately sabotage every relationship, shutting out everyone. There was no help when it got worse, and I began praying for an escape plan. But I was on an island with no way off, and I would not leave without all four children.

The cycle of abuse is horrific. After an abuser becomes emotionally, verbally, or physically violent, they experience self-directed guilt. They then apologize, saying, "I'm sorry for hurting you." They'll bring you gifts, take you on dates, or turn on the affection.

Both the victim and the abuser will rationalize the abuser's behavior by passing responsibility to the victim, saying the victim said or did something to cause the act of violence, using words like, "worthless" or "you made me do it." The abuser completes the cycle with promises to stop or not do it again if the victim would try better.

But that's not the end. The victim will do something to irritate the abuser, the abuser will reflect on all past instances, adrenaline builds, and the abuser becomes enraged. The abuser sets up the victim for some action justifies his rage.

This continues until the victim leaves, and if they don't, the abuse will continue until it brings no satisfaction to the abuser. When the abuser grows immune, they will always take it a step further, until it grows completely physical and ultimately could lead to the victim's death.[1]

Jay completely bypassed emotional and verbal abuse and became physical. One evening, I was boiling chicken for dinner and forgot to take the skin off the chicken. He hated skin on the chicken. When Jay came home from work, he lifted the lid to the boiling hot water and looked at the chicken. He grabbed it out of the boiling water and threw it at me with disgust. He continued reaching into the pot, throwing boiling hot water and chicken at me, burning my chest and neck.

Searing with pain, I ran outside and hid in the small dog shed. I huddled there on the dirty floor, backed into a corner like a beaten dog, insignificant and small. Again, I waited in the silence, in tune with every slight sound. I heard the doors lock.

Realizing I left the kids in there with him alone, I frantically ran back toward the sliding glass door, pounding and begging for him to let me in. My oldest son came to the glass window. We stared at each other for a moment. Then, with a quick motion, he unlocked the slider and let me inside.

Jay came from the hall, grabbing him, shaming him for taking my side, screaming bloody betrayal, telling him he wasn't even my son. He threw him in his room, then slammed the door shut and began beating him. I stood outside the door, pleading with Jay to stop until my throat was dry.

In between the abuse, all I could do was survive. Trying to stay happy, rationalizing and believing our entire family was "perfect." Building a world that was convincing and proving daily that none of it mattered.

Jay began working longer hours, and he used it as an excuse to come home late. It didn't matter to me, because our home was peaceful when he was gone. And when he did come home, he would bring gifts, affirming words of love and kindness. He planned weekly family fun days and was much more affectionate toward me.

In 2008, my oldest daughter had moved back to the mainland to be with her father. Jay offered to get me a ticket so I could fly over for a visit. This was an unusual gift, and I did not hesitate to use it.

Deep down, I knew Jay was having an affair. I didn't have the emotional capacity to question him, giving him space to stay married to me while continuing to sleep with another woman. I truly believed he would come to realize the pain he was causing our marriage, and that, eventually, all things would be made new again.

While away on the trip, Jay rented out an apartment and set up our home as a "common house," inviting his lover into our family home. Jay told the boys that she was a massage therapist. He told the woman that he and I were no longer together, concocting an elaborate story of how we used the home for the kids to stay in when we alternated visitation with them.

At the end of my vacation, he called and told me he wanted a divorce. My world flipped upside down. Caught in an undertow of religious beliefs, isolation from family and friends, fear of losing the kids, and having been ripped of all financial access, I was afraid to stay and I was afraid to leave.

He had convinced me that there was nothing and no one that could love me the way he did. I lived indebted to him for so long that him wanting a divorce caused great fear. I got on the first flight back to the Kauai to show him I could do better.

After arriving home, I found Jay already moved out and into an apartment. The tension between us grew. There were times he would come by the house at night, intoxicated. Sometimes brought gifts. I never knew what to expect, and his behavior sucked me in—until one time I noticed one gift was lingerie from his lover. She was receiving letters and gifts that had once been for me. He was so mixed up in his lies, he often forgot who had been given what and where he had been.

One night he came by and asked me to go out, crying and apologizing for everything. He softened, and I took this as an opportunity to question his motives. Angered by the question, he lunged at me, swinging his fist toward my face. I turned my head to the side, causing his fist to only graze my cheek and go through the wall.

He left the room, slamming the door and trapping me in a space with no exit but the window. I ran across the room and slipped myself out the window. I headed toward the carport and locked myself in the car while calling my mom on the phone. Jay came out, punching and kicking the hood of the car, screaming at me. My mom picked up, hearing everything. With both of us crying on the phone, she begged me to let her call the police.

But I made her promise she wouldn't, because it would make everything worse. Police would only separate us, and Jay would come back with a vengeance. I ended the call, promising her everything had settled down. I lied, telling her he was gone.

I looked at him through the windshield, made eye contact, and asked him to leave me alone. But he was far too angry, and when I refused to get out of the car, he threatened to use the children.

He turned around and went back inside. I was afraid of what he might do, so I got out of the car and went in after him. I don't remember much of what happened after that, except I was in the bathroom once again, curled up in the bathtub, with only a flimsy shower curtain protecting me. The shower was on and running over me, a watery baptism cleansing years of abuse. Crying out to God, I begged, "Get me out or kill me before I die."

The next day I went to church. I did have a few female friends, but kept them on the down low, afraid of what Jay would say or do to sabotage the relationships. He believed any woman who would hang out with me was a slut or bad influence. Church was a safe environment that brought very few questions or arguments, and didn't escalate the tension between us.

The people at church were beginning to ask questions, and when they did, I stopped attending for a while, coming back again when it felt safe. This Sunday, Jay got up to go with me. Unsure of his motive, and concerned someone would see me and ask what happened, with my swollen eyes from crying and a bruised cheek, I concealed the damage with a pair of sunglasses.

When worship started and Jay threw his arms up in the air to praise God, I flinched. This gave me an acute awareness I never had before. How could this man could use the same hands to both worship God and hit me?

The realization sent me into a whirlwind of pain, and I started crying. Afraid he would get angry, I went to the front and laid my head down on the floor in prayer. Praying for God to release me and give me strength to leave. Praying that my life would matter to others and give me purpose to continue living.

While I was praying, a warm and kind woman knelt next to me. She whispered words of power, saying, "I know what he is doing to you. You can get out." Then she prayed for me, and in that prayer she told me I mattered and I was valued. She finished her prayer, rose, and left.

I remained there a long time, trying to process all that had just gone on. Afraid to get up, afraid of what Jay might know, afraid the whole thing was a setup for more pain. But most of all, I was afraid she was telling the truth. What if I mattered after all?

7

THE LIE: I CAN DO IT ON MY OWN - PART 1

"For the Lord God will hold your right hand saying unto you,
fear not I will help you." Isaiah 41:13

I BEGAN PLANNING A WAY OFF THE island. Having all the kids with me was going to make it very difficult. Afraid of the fury within Jay, I went undercover as I searched for help. There were women in the church, a couple more women on the island, and my family that he allowed me to reach out to.

Using cryptic words, I asked for their help, then waited, trusting these women to find a way out. Praying every day for a speedy process.

Within weeks, I received plane tickets for me and all the children. A woman who was an old family friend of ours gave them to us—offering them up with no idea what they were for. Others offered places to stay on the mainland until we reached our destination, which was my mom's one-bedroom apartment.

Emotionally, I prepared myself, digging deep within and looking for strength to follow through. I prayed a lot and read scripture, reminding myself that God was the one in control. I knew the only way I was ever going to get on the plane was by leaving everything behind. Clothing, furniture, photos, and memorabilia—I had to let it all go.

The only thing left to do was come up with a story that Jay would agree with, allowing all the kids and me to get on that plane. Waiting for the "cool down" period, the period of peace. Quieting myself until I knew he wanted to spend time with the other woman.

Earlier in the year during the separation, we had made plans to move back to the mainland. I used this as an excuse to go, asking him if I could take all the kids to visit their sister, my oldest daughter, and while doing so, I would scout out places to live.

Knowing he wouldn't pay for the trip, I told him my family was willing to pay for it all. He agreed. I let a few days go by before I came back with printed plane tickets.

October of 2009. Four backpacks with a week's worth of clothes, four blankets, four of their favorite stuffed animals, and my four children. Jay drove us in the van to the airport.

My body went into physical stress, heart rate rising in panic. My face flushed. Afraid of giving myself away, I turned on some music for distraction while Jay drove us to the airport.

We walked through the small airport toward the gate. Jay was saying goodbye to the kids, and I was trembling as I fumbled for the tickets, nauseous and fearful he would suddenly discover the plan. Forcing myself to turn around and wave, I felt dizzy as we walked through the line and onto the plane.

It wasn't until we were seated and the door to the plane shut that I let out a long sigh of relief. But the first leg of the flight was not without worry. I was in fear the entire time, believing he would somehow stop me, or have someone intercept us when we arrived.

The plane landed, allowing only fifteen minutes to catch our connecting flight while herding four kids ranging in ages of four to ten. We ran with bags and blankets, kids crying and tugging at me to slow down. We were the last ones on board the plane.

Our seats were in the far back, and it was a major effort to make it down the aisle in front of everyone while holding back tears. The kids buckled up across from me, and I dropped into my seat in a heap. Holding my head in my hands, I sat there sobbing.

Once the tears wore off, exhaustion set in. I closed my eyes for rest, but the kids woke me, begging for food. Frantically, I searched my purse for snacks, finding a single small bag of peanuts. I asked them all to share the tiny morsels.

The kids were ravenous and promptly asked for more. We had been on a five-hour flight and changed planes with no time for food. This flight offered nothing except drinks, and I knew they were hungry. How would I get the kids through the next three hours? My thoughts spiraled from there as I faced the larger questions. How would I get these kids through the next three days or weeks? How was I supposed to take care of four kids when I had nothing but a week's worth of clothes and pocket change? I longed to go back home. I couldn't do it without him!

The flood gates opened again, leaving me silently sobbing in the back of the plane.

There was a woman sitting across from me and near the kids. Looking at me with shock, or maybe pity or something in between, she leaned over and whispered, "I have food, honey. I can give your kids the food in my bag." My only response was to nod my head, her voice trailing off in the distance. She talked about being a grandmother and how difficult it was to travel with children.

I prayed to God, asking him for peace. God brought me into beautiful sounds of distant memories. I could hear my mother playing the church piano, my grandmother praying for us by name, my dad giving me loving wisdom. Breaking through the nostalgic memories, a male voice spoke. I hadn't even realized I was sitting next to someone on the plane.

His voice was gentle and kind, the voice of a father, nurturing me with words of care and concern. Affirming me with a Father's love that was endearing and powerful. I do not remember all he said, but he gave me a peace and promise to keep me pressing into God's love. It was all I needed to keep moving toward safety.

After we landed, our friends picked us up. We stayed the night, then caught another flight to my hometown where we were met by some family members. Over the next month, all five of us stayed in a one-bedroom apartment.

Once again, I was in my hometown, sleeping on the couch, with no money or job, emotionally numb, and having a hard time making decisions for the children and myself.

Jay called, first with compliments and then threats. Without me being physically near him, the verbal abuse accelerated. My heart and mind yo-yoed, up and down, like I was his personal emotional playground. On the upswing, he drew me in, petting my ego, and then affirming me with his undeniable love. Using words like, "I love you," "it is my fault," "I care for you" and "I don't blame you," "I am sorry," "you don't deserve any of this," "you are a good woman," and "I need you."

Then the yo-yo dropped, throwing me down with words like, "fuck you," "I cannot stand you," "I hate you," "I don't know why I had a kid with you," "I should have left you when the baby died," "you are meaningless," "nobody will want you," "you're crazy." Most of the messages would be in the same hour, within the same day.

Jay had access to all the finances, including our bank accounts and the children's social security income. Although the kids were with me, they technically lived in Hawaii. It was difficult getting a rental, getting the children into school, and starting a life while financially connected to Jay through marriage.

When Jay realized I was not coming back to the island, he became hostile. He used the finances, threatening our survival, while I waited for him to agree to the decisions.

Mentally sick and exhausted from the constant barrage of verbal abuse hurled at me, I went out one night to get a break. Dressed up and ready to meet some friends at the bar, somewhere in between leaving the apartment and my old stomping grounds, God spoke to me, telling me to go back to my mother's apartment.

God supercharged my heart, giving me strength. From that night forward, I went into overdrive to save our lives, praying daily for God to guide me.

I knew it wasn't safe for me to remain in my hometown. It held too many temptations and reminders that held me back, so I looked for rentals three hours away in the town called Redding. It was far enough away to start over—safely tucked away from all past connections, but close enough to have family support and visitation.

In faith, I prepared to move. It took two weeks to find a place to live and, without a job, I had to rely on Jay's finances, telling the landlord he would provide monthly care through the boys' social security until I got settled in. I put in the application and prayed to God for Jay to keep his word, hoping the finances felt like enough control over our lives for him to continue helping. It would come at a cost, I knew. I was a slave to his every command.

Within days of turning in my application, the landlord called and said I could move in. It was a cute little three-bedroom home in a neighborhood within walking distance to an elementary school. With the help of my uncle, my grandmother, and a multitude of other family members, we moved.

November 1st, 2009, was the first time I walked through the house, overwhelmed with gratitude and nervous about the future. It was beautiful and clean, and they had stocked the fridge full of fresh food. The home had a closed-in backyard and a neighborhood full of children.

My grandmother brought some prayer oil with her and anointed every doorway, praying for me and my children.

Grandma was an only child from the state of Oklahoma. She moved to California in high school, married my grandfather, and had five children. She was a Baptist, strong in her faith, and a mighty intercessor.

I never got to meet my grandpa Joe; he died in a tragic accident. She told me the story, how she ran out the door with all five kids in tow because Joe had forgotten his lunch. He was helping a neighbor down the road, and it wasn't far. As she drove down the road, she saw the tractor had rolled over in a ravine. Telling the kids to stay in the car, she ran to him. Holding her dying husband in her arms, she prayed over him, watching him take his last breath. A bird came down and settled there with them. Grandma said the Holy Spirit came in that moment.

My grandmother's life was turned upside down that day, and she has had a multitude of things happen in her life that would have given her good cause to step outside of her faith. But she pressed in further and deeper with every tribulation, setting a foundation for me to live by.

Every night, grandma prayed faithfully, calling out every family member by name, seventy plus more of us. She prayed for strangers and invited many into her home, including me. I lived with her for a while after I graduated from high school.

She was the quintessential grandmother, teaching me how to sew, cook, and how to care for a home. But most of all, she taught me how to pray. Having my grandma travel three hours out of her way to pray over my home marked me. I held on to that day in times of deep pain when I could not find the strength to pray for myself.

Once my family returned home, I had to fend for myself as a single mother of four children, living in a new town.

The kids were registered in their new schools, and I was alone five full days a week with no friends or family. My thoughts drowned me—like a huge wave, it took me out, rolling me in an undertow of lies. I became aware that I was in an abusive marriage.

When the waves settled, it was quiet and very still, and that is when deception, abuse, and emotional control all surfaced. I had covered it up with a busy life and honeymoon moments of goodness, but the stillness of a healthy home revealed its truth.

Everything came up. The mental anguish was debilitating and took a toll on me. The first few months, I was going through the motions of life. I stopped eating and was barely drinking fluids. I rapidly dropped weight; at one point I weighed in at 80 pounds. I was sick from it all. There was a night when the kids were playing on the couch, building a fort with the cushions. My oldest daughter was calling out to me, but I was having a hard time answering. The noise of the room closed in, becoming an echo as the room spun. The next thing I knew, I woke up with my children standing around me. I had passed out in front of them.

With my health deteriorated, my family decided my stepmom should move in. It was exactly what I needed to gain my strength back and make healthier decisions, but I was internally struggling with the idea that I was failing at being able to do it on my own.

My dad gave me the name of a local church in Redding to attend. It had an exceptional children's program, and I could drop my kids off, giving me some time to myself. I would attend their service and stand at the back each week. A Sunday just before Thanksgiving, they passed a prayer card around. Usually, I let them go by. I struggled asking for help, believing that I could do it all on my own. Relinquishing myself to receiving help meant allowing control into my life again.

This time, I held the card in my hands, gathering the strength to write a few short sentences about our situation. I found the courage to write about our situation, the lack of furniture, finances, and food. I simply asked for help. I wrote my name and number on the card and threw it in the basket.

About a week later, there was a knock on our door. A group of people had gathered furniture, clothing, gift cards, games, and holiday food for our home. I cried that day. They showed up at my door, handing me hope with every gift.

With every act of hope, my health started to return.

Jay called relentlessly, but with my health on the rise, so was my confidence. When my confidence levels rose, so did his threats. He threatened to keep the money that cared for his children; he threatened to take me to court and take the boys away from me; he threatened to follow me. And his threats were working. With every step forward, he pushed me ten steps back, and I felt trapped.

I was afraid to meet new people, convinced they knew him and that their willingness to meet up with me was a ploy to check up on me. If they were from Hawaii or had visited there, I would shut down. I trusted no one and was living in a state of anxiousness and paranoia daily around anyone who approached me.

Often, I wondered if he had flown into town and was following me around. The paranoia was constant, and I was desperate for help. Twice, I drove down the road toward the local domestic violence shelter, and both times I turned away out of fear they would have to contact him. To me, living on an island was not far enough away. His control over me was fierce.

One day, while driving to the grocery store, a JJ Heller song came on the radio. "Your Hands." The lyrics declared that God's hands hold us steady when our world shakes. God spoke to me through that song. With new courage I did not have before, I drove over to the shelter and walked in.

I sat with a woman, a stranger, yet she knew exactly what I was going through—afraid, insecure, and broken. Finally feeling safe, it was everything I needed to gain the strength for a restraining order, divorce, and custody.

Going through a divorce was difficult; it literally took a village of support. I felt an immense amount of failure and shame when it came time to sign the documents. But despite all I had gone through, I grieved my marriage ending. All I ever wanted was to be loved and carry the honor of a marriage lasting until death do us part.

For some, coming out of abuse is like a pendulum. One side of the pendulum is held by entrapment and control, and when it is released, it swings hard and fast the other way toward complete freedom.

At church, there was a small group called Celebrate Recovery. It laid the foundation I so desperately needed, and it was there I met two or three women who became very important to me. But with very little trust in people—and with the idea of having to fit into the rigid role of a Christian woman—the meetings weren't sustaining me.

I looked online for bars near me. I wanted to socialize. One establishment was within walking distance, so I started going once or twice a week. It was exhilarating. This was a new place, no one knew me, and I could be myself. No hiding behind some made up character or label, just drinking beers and dancing.

I made quite a few friends in only a few months. Walking in the door, they called out my name, cheered, and hugged me tight. We became a pack, and often our entire entourage moved from one bar to the next. I was having the time of my life, and many of these people are still some of my closest friends today.

8

THE LIE: I CAN DO IT ON MY OWN - PART 2

In February 2010, I joined some friends at a local sports bar. When I entered, the door glass caught a beam of sunlight, lighting me up like a spotlight on a movie star arriving for a premier.

There was a man sitting with two other men at a table across the way, and I caught his attention. As soon as I was seated, he approached me with a huge smile and lots of charm.

"Hey, you're not from around here. I really like your dreads and your tattoos."

He introduced himself as Cody, followed by a brief conversation that ended as quickly as it began. He turned and went back to his table of friends.

The people I was with knew him and told me he was much younger than me—sixteen years younger. He was known for his wild nature, and they warned me to stay away from him. My compassion toward the "underdog" has always been a prominent force in my life. Therefore, their cautioning me to stay away became my persistence to move toward him. Curiosity rose as I watched him move through the room.

Near the end of the evening, he was playing pool with an older woman. They were laughing and carrying on with genuine affection toward each other. I watched him slide his hand down the small of her back and guide her toward the door to leave.

Something deep inside me surfaced—jealousy—and it caught me off guard. God stirred my heart toward this stranger. It was uncomfortable and disorienting, causing further curiosity. Years later, I found out the women he left with was his aunt.

I had no desire to pursue intimacy, incapable of committing to a relationship. The abuse I endured, and was continuing to endure, shattered all trust I had in people, most of all myself.

Weeks later, I was out at the bar near my home and ran into him once again.

This time I approached him, and we ended up hanging out for most of the evening. We had so much fun, forming an immediate friendship through connection and laughter. Going home that night brought the most peace I had felt in friendship for nearly all my life. I looked him up on social media, sent him a private message, and invited him over for lunch.

He accepted, and from that moment on, he was a part of my daily life. A deep platonic friendship developed, instigated by humor and care. We told each other everything without reservation. Sharing all our life stories with each other until all hours of the night, the walls of distrust toward men began to crumble as I gained trust in his friendship.

One evening in early spring, we were lying underneath a massive Valley Oak we called "The Majestic," staring at the stars through moonlit branches, entwined in blankets on an old trampoline. Sharing our innermost thoughts, fears, and feelings.

There was much respect given to the topic of celibacy. Cody was a complete gentleman; it was raw and vulnerable for both of us to talk about our deepest and personal convictions. That night, the final brick of distrust toward men fell in a heap of dust. Feeling whole once again from the fruit of our friendship sent by God healed parts of me I believed to be gone forever.

As a single mother of four and just out of an abusive marriage, it was difficult to balance my social life. A desired change in my life was to keep focus on my children. They were my responsibility above all else.

One of the most endearing attributes of Cody was his love of children—not having any of his own, and being only 21 years of age to my nearly 37.

There was a Fourth of July event happening in town, for drinking age only. There was food, music, fireworks, and most of my friends were going, but I had to stay home with my kids. As much as Cody wanted to go, he also didn't want me and the kids to be alone on Independence Day.

He surprised us with our own party, bringing blankets from the house and placing them all up on the roof. We had a picnic and watched the fireworks together. This was one of many adventures, deepening and building our friendship. Over time, we danced in the rain, swam in the dark, played hide and seek in the neighborhood, and had many full days at the lake.

We were adults with childlike spirits. There was no discipline to it; we were unstoppable. I'd never been able to build trust in a relationship like this with a man before, but with him, there was a level of communication and loyalty I'd never experienced, and it was unexpected.

Often, the both of us exchanged endearing words. It was a friendship that felt like the love of family, and saying I love you to each other was a symbol of it all. Midsummer of 2010, we were at a friend's home for a pool party. Cody and I were in the pool, leaning against the side in the shade, watching our friends splash about.

He turned to me and said, "I love you." It was so matter of fact and filled with such genuine love, it terrified me. Everything about him felt safe, and this type of deliberate "I love you" historically symbolized future pain and rejection to me. Conflicted, something inside of me wanted to say it right back, but instead, I ran, spending the rest of the afternoon literally locked in the bathroom battling it out.

Two of my close friends rotated in and out of the bathroom, trying to convince me that his love was real. They saw something pure between us and begged me to go back out there and say yes to Cody's love. I was in a tug of war between past, present, and future, scared and convinced that I was no good to anyone anymore and meant to live a life of doing everything on my own.

Days went by, and things between us returned to normal. I was having a BBQ with immediate family and friends, standing beneath the Majestic oak tree, when Cody knelt in front of me. In front of everyone, he professed his love to me once again, asking me to be his girlfriend.

My first response was reminding him of my past, the divorce I was still going through, and the four children that were my priority, about how young he was, and how he deserved a fresh start in his life with children of his own. I just knew one of us would end up hurt.

He responded, "I know what I want, and I know what God is telling me I deserve." The man was relentless in his pursuit of me. With a new heart and new hope, I said yes. And, from that day forward, we turned one of the greatest friendships into an authentic love story.

Walking in a new heart toward love did not mean I was all in. Yes, I wanted to be, but there was a battle between staying in a relationship and wanting to run from the inevitable. I prayed daily for answers, wanting to know if it was God's will in my life. I wanted to do nothing outside of Him.

God continued to show up, and visions of Cody danced through my thoughts. My spirit lifted, peace surrounded me, and He said, "This is my promise to you, to awaken love, press into its promise." There were many things that drew me near to Cody, and through it all, my heart changed and love grew.

We were driving down the road during a hot summer afternoon. I turned on one of my favorite James Taylor albums. Throwing my hand out the window and surfing the oncoming summer breeze, I sang.

James Taylor was way before my time, but my parents raised me listening to him. He was one artist who eased my pains and brought me back to the days I lived in freedom. Turning on his music, I would disappear into memories of driving down the Redwood Highway with the top off my car, singing to the heavens above in the most carefree days of my life.

The song, "Fire and Rain" came on. Cody began singing along in a strong voice. I looked over at him singing a song that brought me so much peace over the years and wondered how a man sixteen years younger than me knew this song.

The sun caught the corner of his half-down window, and the ever-faithful sunbeam showed up, shimmering on his right cheek. Then, something real woke in me—love awakened. I was all in that day, pressing into the promise of God's love.

About a year later, Cody and I went on a week-long vacation to discover the Northwest. One of the places was Helena, Montana. A nearby college was having an fall event—a major symphony, with a well-known violinist. The college organized everything. You bring canned food for their local food drive and a quilt, placing all the food on all four corners of your blanket to be picked up throughout the night. It was stunning, the entire campus lawn and hillside covered in hundreds of blankets, giving a visual of one giant patchwork quilt.

The music started at sunset, and Cody and I moved up to the front row to have the best view of the symphony. Hand in hand, we walked along the lawn, stopping and talking with people and really taking it all in.

Cody was raised in the country, and sports, not music, was his area of expertise at the time. He had never been to theatre, let alone a symphony. Watching him experience classical music was intriguing. Every time they violinist played, he clapped with as much enthusiasm as a touchdown at a football game. It was both fascinating and uncomfortable for me.

In his enthusiasm, Cody suddenly stood up and grabbed me, pulling me with him. Throwing his arms around my waist, everything disappeared as we slowed danced to the sounds of a symphony in front of hundreds of people. I looked up into the darkness of the night, smiling. There was no sunbeam glistening, but there were a million stars winking, giving their promises of love.

God's faithful sunbeam showed up only one more time for me. Cody and I went on a trip to a town called Trinidad on the coast of California. We regularly made trips to the coast, staying in a small cabin near the ocean, walking the beach looking for rocks and shells, and sometimes stopping to stare at the crashing waves while Cody played his guitar.

This weekend was raining hard, but we continued along the beach hand in hand. Suddenly the rain turned to snow. It was a genuine phenomenon; it was highly unusual to snow in Trinidad. Here we were, standing on a beach with snowflakes floating down around us.

Neither of us had experienced anything like it, and we laughed and cried out in its magnificent glory. We were dancing around taking it all in, when the clouds parted briefly, and a beautiful sunbeam with an array of color shone down right on us both. The faithful sunbeams that used to show when I was beaten down, desperate, and wanting pain to end, now became sunbeams mending the broken and showing the way.

I never dreamt I could love a man this much. Standing there under the sunbeam, arms stretched out toward Heaven, embracing the snowy white delicate miracles floating all around us, my heart wept with true love.

Four years into dating, our relationship took a turn. Drinking and going out together was no longer fun. We were arguing a lot, and I was growing increasingly convicted about my life. Reminded often of all that God wanted for me and my family, I slowed down and prayed daily for our relationship to shift toward His will in our life.

Cody and I attended church often and consistently showed up for Celebrate Recovery meetings. We both talked about God, even bringing Him into our discussions when we were out at night. As a team, we had a powerful draw toward God, but I was convicted of our lifestyle, and I turned every conviction on Cody, wanting more out of him than he saw in himself. But compelling someone toward the vision you see in them is unhealthy, and it impedes the choice of free will and hearing God's voice directed toward their journey together.

In prayer, God showed up and shared with me all past blessings and answered prayers. He gave me new vision for the future. Continuing to affirm me, God and I built a strong relationship, walking and talking for hours. I wrote a journal of all our conversations.

Around 3:00 a.m. on an evening in 2013, God woke me up with a gentle voice and asked me to write something down. Titled, "A Glimpse Into The Future," I underlined it. Below the title I wrote, "NOTHING is as it seems," followed by a surge of scripture.

This journal entry never made sense to me; I tried to share it many times with people, calling my grandma, asking her what she thought of it all, always with the same answer—nobody understood it. Bringing it to Cody as well, but something always got in the way, so I finally ended up tucking it away.

In 2014, we broke up. Breaking up this time was different. It wasn't desperate, but it hurt like a deep, searing wound. I didn't want it to happen, because we belonged, but knew it had to happen because we were unhealthy. The first three days of the breakup, I did not even get out of bed. It took a few friends coming over and literally yanking me out of the covers, throwing me in the shower, and giving me a life lecture for me to get motivated once again.

Starting fresh, I moved into a new place, got a job, and focused on my relationship with God. I grew deeply enriched with Him like never before. I read scripture daily, prayed over my kids and myself, twice daily sent Cody scripture, reminding him he belonged to God, but never interfering in the process that he would have to go through.

A few months after we broke up, God met me in my dreams, saying, "Remember that journal you wrote? Go get it." I pulled it out of its tucked-away place and read, "A Glimpse Into The Future, NOTHING is as it seems." What I once couldn't understand, became very clear at that moment.

It said,

"Though you go through hard times, you are still elected to foreknowledge of God. God has his eye on us, and He is determined by the work of the Spirit to keep us obedient through Christ. Reality of pain does not diminish what we have, which is Living Hope. Being grieved by trial is temporary and good faith to be tested."

I was in awe! God was preparing me for our breakup.
The journal entry also stated our relationship was Imperative.

"A relationship that expresses an unavoidable obligation, a necessity. God is faithful to our glimpse of the future, but nothing is as it seems when that glimpse is given."

My heart leapt with joy as I continued reading and understanding what lie ahead for us both.

God gave me commands to follow. I wrote,

"Get ready for action, avoid distorted thinking, set hope in His grace, be obedient, do NOT give in to your former ways! Cody, rejoice in hope and patient tribulation with steadfast prayer. Rita, believe the love God sent and perfect love casts out fear."

God was restoring us through the process of a breakup, giving me a glimpse into the future, and allowing me to see His mighty and perfect plan in our lives.

I wrote Cody a letter that night, fully letting go of him. Knowing that God was in every part of his life and would be in every part of healing our relationship. God transformed me, preparing me for what was to come.

During the breakup, I switched churches and began attending The Stirring. One Sunday, the pastor, Nathan Edwardson, was giving the sermon. Just like I always did, I stood in the back, head low and undetected. But one time, I briefly looked up and caught a glimpse of his shoes. He was wearing "Chucks," Converse tennis shoes. As an avid skateboarder, this intrigued me.

His shoes strengthened my intention to listen carefully, and by the end of the sermon, his shoes gave me the boldness to walk down that aisle and introduce myself. In conversation, I found out both of us had four children and liked skateboarding. It was the very first time I entered a significant church culture I could relate to, one where I could authentically walk into a building and find acceptance right where I was at, without judgment or law over my life. The Stirring has been my home church and loyal community since 2014.

A lot of difficult changes began happening to our family.

In a matter of months, Jay moved to Redding, fought for the kids in court, and then turned around and moved back to Hawaii. It shook the foundation I built, invaded my safe environment, and brought with him all my old fear patterns. I was crumbling under anxiety, believing everything he said I was once again.

Showing up to court the first time was one of the most courageous things I had to do, coming face to face with someone who had a hold on my life. I was shaking, dizzy, and near passing out, but I did it. I stood there in court, boldly stating the truth despite the consequences. The truth always costs something, but the lies had cost me so much more.

After it was over, the bailiff escorted Jay out. When we reached the steps, he turned to me and I finally made eye contact with him. Always knowing this moment would come, I had so much to say, so much anger raging inside. But there I stood, looking him in the eye, saying, "I forgive you." He walked away, and I sat down on the cement steps of the courthouse and sobbed. It was the freest I had felt in a long time.

Jay only stayed in Redding for a short time. During his time of visitation, he significantly influenced our oldest son by writing him letters that spoke detrimental lies about me and the kids. Jay wanted our oldest son to believe that his adoption wasn't valid and I had kidnapped him. It caused so much mental anguish in the home; I took it to court. It was a story so uncannily similar to the one he told to me when we met that I wondered if his ex-wife had been abused as well.

The judge ordered Jay to stop speaking to the kids in any way that had to do with me or the divorce, but that wasn't enough to keep him from saying what he wanted. Our oldest son's behavior shifted drastically. He was becoming physically violent with me and acting out in school.

At one point, he ran away. And so when he asked to move back to Hawaii with his dad, I said yes. Praying daily for his heart, hoping I was making the right decision, I drove him to the airport. It was a long and gut-wrenching drive. How far we had come from escaping it all, and now I was driving him right back into the storm.

I grieved for my son, not wanting him to go. My love for him rose beyond measure, memories popping up in my thoughts like a movie reel. I cried with every minute passing as I walked my son through the airport in silence. I said goodbye. He turned toward the gate to leave and never looked back. Everything moved around me, people's lives going. It was all insignificantly unmatched to the pain I felt in my heart. My head spinning, I collapsed right in the middle of the walkway of the airport.

My youngest son followed his brother a few years later, with less tension. Soon after, my oldest daughter moved in with her father three hours away—back to our hometown so she could finish out her high school years. By the end of 2014, it was just my youngest daughter and me.

With nearly all my children moving out of the home, I felt failure, but my love for them was unwavering, and I kept faith, trusting in God and what He would do for my kids, weighing in hope for them all to come back home.

With the boys living with Jay, he used them as a new control tactic. In order for me to talk to the boys, I would have to go through Jay, and it terrorized me.

Trying to go around him, I called the school, but I was unlisted as a parent. The school had a poor report of me on file, keeping me from all contact. Taking it to court was not an option at the time, and my oldest son called and asked that I stop reaching out. Christmas and birthday gift boxes kept getting returned, hate mail showing up.

Jay's girlfriend was sending letters to me, emails, text messages, and phone calls with hang-ups or threats. Fake social media accounts appeared, and private messages continued to come in with relentless attacks. I was anxious, depressed, and suffering from PTSD. Seeking professional help, I was given a couple of options. One, to have a mediated number to go through, and Jay would not do that. Or, two, cut off all contact, and that came at a hefty cost of not talking to the boys for some time.

My youngest daughter, who was nine years old, was supposed to visit Jay, but she did not want to go. The order of visitation bound us to it, causing her a lot of anxiousness leading up to the flight. Every time there were visits planned, something would come up. Jay would cancel, saying he couldn't afford it or completely changing his mind, thus hurting our kids and causing trust issues within the unreliability.

When it came to our daughter, Jay would not claim her as his own, and told me to keep her when we divorced. The first year we went to court, she was unlisted as a child in his request for custody. He told me she should not have been born, citing the first miscarriage as a lesson.

He did not believe she was his child and demanded a paternity test, something he also did to his ex-wife with their youngest son. He was a patterned abuser, adamantly wanting to talk to her, sending her gifts, writing her letters. And then, just as adamantly, he exposed her to his doubts, alluding to the lies, and threatening her through text messages. It was making her sick. So, when it came time for her to fly by herself to see him, she did not want to go.

I knew Jay still had the girlfriend in his life. The last time she and I spoke was in 2010, when she called me and asked me if Jay and I were still married. Jay had lied to her about everything, and I told her the truth, asking her to leave us alone. Despite the possibility of divorce, it was not her business to be in our lives. I told her if she chose to go back to him, she would lose my respect and I wouldn't speak to her ever again.

But the kids told me they cared for her. She was kind and had a soft demeanor, and so I leaned on that with every visitation. It was the only safety I had in allowing my daughter to go, and she was leaving for her dads in a few short days.

We were packing for her trip. It was chaotic and messy, and I asked her several times to do a chore. It always took her time to do any chore, often getting sidetracked, dancing around like a fairy in circles. She was a rainbow and butterflies girl, invariably floating away in her vivid imagination.

After asking several times for her to do the chore, I turned toward her and, in a firm voice, repeated myself. She pointed at something, then suddenly dropping to the ground. Assuming she was playing, I told her to get up, but then I noticed her violently shaking, spitting, and her face was turning blue. I thought she was dying.

I screamed out bloody murder for help and called the emergency operator, not knowing if she had hit her head earlier in the day, taken some poison, or if she was choking. Yelling at the emergency operator, I pleaded for anyone in the apartment complex who could hear me to come help.

Suddenly, a man came out of nowhere, picking my daughter up and lying her on the couch. She became very still. I was sobbing and crying out. Was she dead? In a coma? The man leaned over and began praying, speaking a language I did not understand.

She woke up but did not know who I was. The man turned to me and said, "Your daughter sees angels. She is close to God. Never let anyone tell you otherwise." And then he left right as the ambulance arrived. She became more aware, sitting up and saying, "I saw an angel in a far-off place."

I never saw that man again, but we believe to this day that God sent him.

From that time, my daughter was actively having multiple seizures and received a diagnosis of epilepsy. With every passing day, I felt defeat. There had been too much, and my mind refused to stay strong any longer. I lived in a constant state of fight or flight, an acute stress response. I was suffering from PTSD. Lying awake at night with anxiety. When I finally fell asleep, I'd wake up kicking, screaming, and crying.

I also struggled with Obsessive Compulsive Disorder most of my life, my mind working to control the out-of-control environment around me. Everything had to be orderly and clean, with specific places for each item in my home, panicking if things were moved out of place. Leaving or returning from home had a routine, and volume on phones, radios, or television had to be set at even numbers.

One of the most debilitating compulsions became the restroom. Anxiousness upset my stomach and caused several humiliating accidents; these accidents led me to insistent searching for a nearby restroom. When showing up at new places, I would find the restroom before doing anything. It was a vicious cycle. If there was no restroom, I would panic. The panic irritated my bowels, which cause me to need the restroom. As a result, I stopped going most places.

With all these things happening—and with my daughter being diagnosed with epilepsy—my flight or fight response shifted into overdrive. My out-of-control life activated the control button in me—or my wish for one.

I lashed out at God, cussing, shouting, pounding the steering wheel when driving down the road. Sometimes I fell to my knees in the gravel while out on a walk, screaming for peace. I wanted out of it all. The only time of peace was at church, in community, listening to worship, finding hope through testimonies and the Word of God. I continued to stay the course and listen for God's will in my life.

About the same time, Cody had a life-changing encounter with God. We began hanging out again, and by the beginning of 2015, we were back together. Coming back together was a more beautiful experience. We cherished each other more, there was a drive to stay sober, learn about God, what He was doing independently in our lives, and we worked harder to grow in our relationship as our lives grew in God.

The change in us was radical and happened quickly with news that we were pregnant in August, engaged by September, and married in November. After five years of dating, God was working on Cody's heart toward marriage. He bought an engagement ring, letting it sit in his truck for months before he proposed. The proposal was beautiful, a cherished moment in my hometown on the beach where I grew up, with both my daughters there as witnesses.

Saying yes to Cody was easy. God drew us in to each other, and I saw our forever together. Yet, there was so much apprehension about how good it was. Afraid of the rug of goodness being pulled out from under me, I disconnected from it all. While planning the wedding, I was aware of how much it mimicked my marriage to Jay. Everything moved quickly, and I was pregnant. The similarities were enough to scare me. I wanted to run away before it turned on me.

The unknown and the "what-ifs" were terrifying as I filled each void with a potentially horrifying scene of abuse and control that would play out in our marriage, sabotaging my engagement and the wedding plans.

Spiraling, I called it quits, believing the lie that I could do it all on my own.

God brought two people into my life that changed the course of this lie. Jim Bailey, also a pastor at The Stirring Church, was our officiant. He sat with me in the back of the church café, at a little table on the right-hand side. Right by the window, with streams of light coming through the glass and landing on the table as a reminder of God's loyalty. Jim reminded me that Cody was not Jay, and this marriage was not our story. Everything looked the same because our God is a restorative God and He was taking all things painful and making them new once again.

Still full of fear and ready to back out, I met with our wedding planner, Gwen, Pastor Nate's mom. She sat me down in the same church café and asked me to share my story leading up to the engagement. I was back in time, escaping abuse, catching a flight off the island, seated next to a man on the plane—a fatherly figure praying for me.

She abruptly stopped me right there. The story I was telling her was very familiar. She knew the man who was on that plane. It was her husband, Dale, the father of my pastor. He had told her about a young, blonde, dreadlock girl with her kids on a flight from Hawaii. I could not believe it!

God planned it all, from Dale being on the plane that day, meeting Cody at the bar, and me showing up at the Stirring Church where Pastor Nate welcomed me. God was putting me in the right places, at the right times, surrounded by the right people.

Sitting there in the café with my pastor's mom, my life had come full circle to this moment. My heart shifted, and fear dissipated. God wanted me to stop running. I wasn't made to do it on my own, and He had a mighty plan for my life—a fully restored future with Cody by my side.

9

THE LIE: I AM DISQUALIFIED

"For God intended that your faith not be established on man's wisdom but by trusting in his almighty power." 1 Corinthians 2:5

OUR WEDDING WAS STUNNING. IT WAS ON November 11th of 2015. We had no wedding party, invited my daughters into the ceremony, and together, hand in hand, we walked each other down the aisle. We received a standing ovation from all those who had stood by us and wanted to invest in what God was doing through us.

We turned the main room of the church into a barn setting, complete with hay bales. Strings of lights above our heads shone on us as we walked down the aisle to worship music. We incorporated a Jewish prayer into the ceremony, and a multitude of people laid hands on us in warm and hopeful prayer.

Our honeymoon was in North Lake Tahoe as a gift from both Dale and Gwen Edwardson, a beautiful apartment with a fireplace and lots of views. We went on drives and took a helicopter ride above the snowy mountains.

Coming home was strange. I wish I could say we lived happily ever after, but that is not the case. On the first morning of marriage, we literally did not know who we were lying next to. A system had been in place, playing house together. Five years of navigating chores, paying bills, work schedules, and sex did not prepare us for the sanctification of entering a covenant. We were strangers to each other. Neither of us were prepared for the heart and desires of each other, nor what it would look like for us to become one in Christ.

In the process of learning how to navigate a new marriage and a pregnancy, we argued a lot—voices rising, things slamming, and ending with Cody taking off. Without proper counsel, these negative encounters easily triggered my past, and I would disassociate or become hostile and fight back. Coming out of abuse and into a new marriage was unexpectedly difficult. I was unraveling at the seams.

Both of us were in sobriety as well. The unaddressed traumas from our past lives profoundly affected our marriage, and we were hurting each other through it all. Cody admitted to not knowing how to be a husband, and I did not feel deserving of his love and goodness, even if he was a loving husband. Our wounds sabotaged peace in our home.

Someone recommended a professional counselor, Doug Porter, a Licensed Marriage and Family Therapist. Seeing Doug was eye opening for us both, and under his guidance, we learned to communicate, connect, and find grace for each other. There was hope for the marriage even in the hardest of times.

One of the things we carried away from therapy was to be intentional with each other. Pray for one another, and view each other as God viewed us. I began understanding the trauma I had endured, learning to identify what PTSD was and how to work through past abuse. Giving voice and understanding to the things from my past began my healing.

Love surrounded our new little daughter from the day of her birth in March 2016. She was the tie that bound all the children together, as well as an answered prayer of her sister. When her sister came to see her for the first time, she could barely breathe through her tears of joy.

I was 43 years old when she was born. Having a child this far along in life brought me both honor and constraint—the joy of celebrating the miracle of having another child, but having to start all over. My freedom was at stake, and this added responsibility was burying the desires of my future. This became the driving force for me to go after my dreams.

I grew up in a Baptist environment. Pretty conservative. Dressed up every Sunday in our best dress, legs crossed, no fidgeting or talking during service. My mom played the piano at the church, and people lined up in hard wooden pews and sang from large brown hymnal books. I always felt like the lucky kid, because I sat in the front where my mom was. Grandma would give me a piece of gum to keep me quiet and focused during the whole service.

The sermon was a full reading of scripture—no stories, or analogies. After church, we would gather in the church kitchen and eat potluck dishes brought from home. The kids played on the lawn and the parents sat around talking about the church, Sunday school classes, sermons, and the next big event coming up.

God was on Sunday; He was a Bible, and it provided rules to live by and morals we emulated. We prayed to Him every night before bed and sometimes before we ate. I heard God and Scripture come up in conversation when someone needed wisdom or salvation.

Since I was a little girl, I have been able to hear the voice of God. I did not know what to do with it since there was no one in my life that talked about hearing from God. I would have *God dreams*, and wake up in the morning to write them down in a journal. He spoke to me about great things He had in store for my life.

Once, when I was about six or seven years old, I took a few New Testament pocket Bibles with me to the end of our street and started waving them at passing cars. As loud as my little voice could yell, I told the story of Jesus and offered free Bibles to anyone who stopped.

I got scolded for it, and a piece of my spirit retreated that day.

In Junior High, we switched to a non-denominational church. I loved it there: the music and small band, the sermons (more enlightening with stories), and the freedom to ask questions during youth group. I journaled every sermon, and brought notes back home to do my own studies. I opened to the thought that we were made for a purpose or a drive to spread the gospel. Christ, for me, became less law and more mission minded.

Ready to be baptized, I asked the pastor if I could participate in the upcoming ceremony. I also asked permission to give a word about what

God was saying for my life. The pastor chuckled a little and asked me to come back with a written paper on why I wanted to be baptized. Once I returned it, he would look it over and let me know.

I was never baptized. And another piece of my spirit retreated under the depths of feeling disqualified.

Yet even with that disappointment, I bounced back. During the peak of my purity years in high school, I carried my Bible everywhere I went, spoke openly of God, went on a couple mission trips, and proudly protected my faith. My life in Christ became oriented toward missions plus teaching. My heart for YWAM (an interdenominational Christian training organization) desired to minster and travel like Jesus did.

I wanted to be a disciple of the gospel. The Bible's teachings captivated me, and I loved teaching others. I wrote an entire Bible study and shared it with our leader, excited to be recognized by leadership and asked if I could lead the next study group.

He said, *"Your study is fantastic, but you do not have the actual life experience to present a topic like this to others."*

I stopped writing and preparing studies. The part of me excited about the teachings of God retreated to feeling disqualified.

After I graduated high school, my goal was to get my Master of Divinity degree, become a pastor, and then head to YWAM. I desired the study of theology, to have skills in leadership, and to have a certification that would present me as qualified for any church. I contacted a nearby college to begin the registration process. They asked what degree I was interested in, and I told them with much confidence.

Their response was: *"Taking the classes to be a pastor would not be beneficial for someone 'like you,' but the church is always in need of administration or daycare providers."*

I disappointment, I dropped everything—YWAM, Bible college, courses, and classes. Being a woman disqualified me from teaching in the church.

All these moments in my life led to deep, wounded feelings of disqualification. As a result, I put the Bible down, only occasionally bringing up God throughout the years, whether through prayer or petitioning of him to get me out of pain.

Regardless, the voice of God entered my dreams often through predictive dreams that would often come true. In a crowd of feisty friends and psychedelics, it was safe to talk about these dreams. They welcomed it. I was called a psychic at one point, a lover of mother earth, and they even named me Shorah, a goddess of the light. In reality, I was lost, but seeking spirituality and truth through false idols labeled me 'qualified.'

Fast forward to fall of 2009, I went to a little coffee shop called Yaks, in Redding, California. I was there just about every day, reading the Bible, surrounding myself in the atmosphere of good people and laughter. There was an older man named Cliff, who everyone knew. I sat with him for hours, sharing our lives with each other. He was the very first person I met in Redding. Cliff saw something in me, and he nurtured it.

Yaks was hiring, but having just arrived in Redding, I wasn't ready to get a job. My kids and I were still traumatized from leaving Hawaii, and starting a new life felt overwhelming. Something pressed me anyway, and I went in for the interview process. About forty people were in the small little café, applying for the same position. There was something about them I had never experienced before, so full of life and it was contagious.

Sitting at a large rectangular table with about ten of them, they openly talking about God. The conversation intrigued me. They spoke of God in a way I had never known. He was not Scripture; he was not an ethical debate or a moral law. God was a part of a discussion, as if joining them at the table.

It was fascinating and drew me in. One person turned to me and asked point blank what my story was. The question was full of kindness, compassion, and with an authority that activated me. I described my situation, telling every emotional detail to that table full of people intently listening with care and desire, and then one of them asked if they could pray for me.

We all joined hands around the table, and one by one, they prayed with power and boldness, praying for my life and my children. As they continued, my hands began to heat up. At one point they became so hot my palms burned. I wanted to pull away, but something was happening inside of me and I did not want it to stop. At about the point where I could no longer stand the relentless heat, the prayer ended. I thanked them and politely excused myself, full of wonder, not knowing right then that the Lord touched me that day.

God kept revealing himself to me in subtle and tangible ways, preparing me for what was to come.

The following year, 2010, Cody invited the kids and me to a holiday dinner at the home of his Uncle Bill and Aunt Beni Johnson. I did not know who his family was, I just knew they were Christians and pastors of a local church. I was nervous.

Jay's abusive words continued to haunt and harass my thoughts, and I was embarrassed at being sixteen years older than Cody—not to mention being in the middle of a divorce, having four kids, disconnected from God, and wearing my past like a scarlet letter.

I drank half a bottle of vodka before I got there just to make it through the night. By the time I arrived, I was intoxicated. Their family was warm and welcoming, almost too much for me to receive while mired in my shame and disqualification.

There was one point in the evening where I was wandering around the home, taking it all in. Their interior balcony overlooked the living room space, and I looked down to see Cody and the kids. Somewhere between drunk and shame, I gave up on the evening and let the mess become me. Without a care, I produced a mock sermon from their balcony and ended it with…

"Don't bring it halfway, bring it *allllllll* the way!"

This was a statement I would make when Cody and I were out at the bars dancing. There was an odd silence in the house, and then everyone continued to their business.

Beni wasn't fazed. She called me into the kitchen, pulled me in close, and gave me the biggest smile. Just like that moment in Yak's, she asked me questions that were compassionate and full of authority. Again, something activated deep within, and I answered her.

Over the years, Beni's questions turned into prayers, and those prayers led to guidance. To this day, besides my grandmother, there has been no other woman who brought me into my greatest potential of faith.

Beni saw me. She saw past the trauma, the addictions, and the single mom going through a divorce. She saw past my mess and saw a daughter of God. She listened and loved. She pushed me to continue when it was hard, and gave me wisdom on how to keep going. She guided me through marriage with honesty and grace, and inspired me to become a wife and mother of faith. She continued to be a nurturing figure in my life until the day she died.

One of the catalytic moments of my faith was around 2011, when Beni invited me to a women's conference at their church. It was a non-denominational church, but more charismatic than I had ever participated in. Going alone—and bringing many questions about God and church—I anticipated receiving answers through others, but God had other plans for me that weekend.

It was rather stagnant during the first couple of days, and I was disappointed—until the final day of the conference. We were in worship, and someone stepped onto the stage to pray. They prayed with such fervor and life, proclaiming words of wisdom and visions from God out to several women in the audience.

They were hearing words from God and inviting his presence into the room. I was in awe at the wonder of it all, and I sensed an immediate awareness of who I was. All the things of my past—the dreams, the "psychic" abilities, the way I felt around certain people and the visions I would have of them—formed into a whole and complete understanding. I had a gift from God. He was with me; He was an invitation and a presence.

Standing and sobbing in the back of the room, I prayed out to God, asking for a word of prayer over my life from the speaker. She kept asking individual women in the group to stand up, and then gave them words of wisdom with prayer. One by one this happened, until the worship ended and the conference was over.

There was a contrasting mixture of disappointment and new revelation over my life as we were ushered out of the building. A woman with long black hair and a warm smile pushed past people, coming toward me. She looked me directly in the eyes and said,

"God wants to know what you want. He said you have cried over many things, but you never tell Him what you want. I cannot leave here until you tell Him."

I was already experiencing the encounter with God, when she gave me a direct word from Him. It was as if God himself stepped out of the box I had placed him in and hugged my heart with His tangible presence. I cried out for mercy and peace. I cried out for forgiveness. I asked for a marriage from Cody, a complete and faith-filled family. And most of all, I surrendered myself to Him, to be all that He wanted me to be.

Also around that time, I met three women (Judy, Nancy, and Victoria) who run a ministry called Truth Ministries Workshop. They guide you out of bitterness and through the process of forgiveness, bringing freedom to your life.

The first time we met, they prayed over me, giving me instructions on how to remove bitterness and resentment, then how to replace it with things of God. It was such an intense process that the first time I did it I panicked. My chest tightened, cutting off my breath. There was so much dark history and many layers that needed to be undone. I could only touch the surface.

Up to the year 2012, I was attending Celebrate Recovery, a place to find freedom from issues controlling your life. I gained a small and consistent faith-based community of people who supported me weekly. Crystal, who became a cherished friend, was a generous prayer warrior, attentive to everything happening in my life. She checked on me, asking about every family member. This beautiful soul encouraged one of the leaders of CR to have me tell my story.

In spite of my early love of theatre, speaking in front of groups traumatized me. Crystal was such a shy and introverted woman, but when she felt God on something, she was powerfully in pursuit of it. I gave in and signed up to speak.

My knees shook as I climbed onto a barstool in front of the small group of people that night. But right as I started speaking, an overwhelming sense of peace washed over me. This was right where I needed to be.

On Easter Sunday of 2014, eleven years to the day that God met me in that dark grungy dive bar, I was at The Stirring Church. They were baptizing people in a portable tank near the stage, and I watched as each person rose and got in line. There was no essay to write, no course you had to go through. It was a beautiful sight.

The group of friends I sat with—some of whom had not been to church until they met me—encouraged me toward the baptismal. They did not understand how I could bring so many to the Lord but not have been baptized myself. And so, I was baptized that day. Easter Sunday.

From 2015 to 2018, I attended women's retreats and a multitude of faith-based classes and conferences. I simply could not get enough.

Stacks of journals covered my bookshelf, full of insight, prayers, words of wisdom, and leadership skills. I was giving out as much as I put in.

I started my own studies, small groups, retreats, and classes. Also writing several courses and even sermons, but tucking them away. There was a fire burning inside of me to be all God designed me to be.

In 2018, I joined a discipleship intensive at The Stirring Church called Emerge. Emerge is a nine-month journey designed to explore, discover, and activate the leader within by embracing your faith and influence. We are assigned a mentor, a small group, and each month we gather as a whole body. The nine months included a deeper life retreat, and ended with a women's (or men's) retreat. As a student, you get out of the journey what you are willing to put into it. It is self-directed and expands your willingness to set aside personal growth and time with God.

My mentor was a woman I had followed and admired tremendously. Pastor Amy Bailey was in a leader in The Stirring Church and director of Emerge. I aspired to be like her, ministering to many with such care and patience. She was both fierce and humble, and could delegate multiple tasks with precise vision, turning Emerge into a beautiful event full of honor and respect. At the same time, she kept her priority of wife and mom at the forefront.

Entering the Emerge season with an energy to be all these things, was great, but it was out of priority for what God was doing in and through my life. When Amy sat with me every week, she encouraged my gifts for discernment and prophecy. But she was also tugging at the pieces of me I wanted to leave behind.

During one of our visits, she encouraged me to tell more of my story. Most people knew I was a survivor, but they did not know *what* I had survived. She wanted me to dig deeper into the details. I was all in for God, my faith growing. I was baptized, leading my own groups, ready to take a step up the leadership ladder. After moving *on* with my life, why did I need to talk about all the things I moved away *from*? I wanted to be seen as strong and well put together. I did not trust anyone to know the battles that I went through. If I was anything less than appearing qualified, I would retreat.

Another part of Emerge showed how to get alone with God *intentionally* and listen for his voice—to get to know Him intimately. I hardly understood what it was to be alone with God. I believed in Him, heard His commands, had dreams and visions, but I did not understand what it meant to surrender my life to Him—to allow God to have every part of my life, or to walk in my gifts. All I understood of God was good works, walking out Christ in action. To me, His voice, the dreams, and visions, were outside of Him, but not inside me by Christ, who is in me.

What Amy was trying to do was surface the pain, clean it out, and allow God to take residence *inside* so He could bring healing. I graduated Emerge with a lot of growth and a great community of people. Even if I did not participate in what God had in store for me, I took a lot away and would later see the seeds Amy planted in my life come to harvest.

I challenged myself in the church by claiming authenticity, but was still feeling deeply disqualified. I knew what I was meant to do, but thought I had to *work* my way to it through people-pleasing and good works. I was motivated from pain, and this created inferiority and comparison, which ultimately led me through a lot of rejection. And with each rejection, I would shrink back into being disqualified.

The only way out was to meet it head on. I sat with each person who I thought rejected me. One woman in our church oversaw the women's ministry. For nearly two years I had a dialogue running in my mind about how different we were, how she saw me, and in it all I believed she disqualified me from ever being able to obtain the position to which God was calling me.

These thoughts and fictional storylines ballooned into feelings of mass rejection. I would often come home crying and carrying offense.

Coming out of Emerge, I desired more. I felt the passion for what God was saying over my life. I saw the gifts and put them to use; however, I lacked God's vision for me. This blurred the lines of what I wanted and where God was leading me.

There was an upcoming women's retreat, and I had a desire to speak. To share words of wisdom through prayer and petition and produce a short teaching point through story and scripture.

So, when the women's retreat leader came up to me and asked me to oversee the fun and games portion of the retreat, it deeply wounded. Stepping into automatic defense mode, I remember looking her in the eye and, with a firm voice, telling her I was more than fun and games— but I would still do it. She was a little taken aback by my response. This woman did not know I had been collecting more than dusty offenses. They were entire dirt clods stuck in my shoe.

During the weeks leading up to the retreat, I heard the Lord telling me to write letters He wanted me to share with some women on the retreat. The first woman was the women's ministry leader. The words I wrote in the letter were all the things I had prayed for personally, words I desired to be spoken and affirmed over my own life.

The day I was called up to read the letter over her was a challenging experience. Here I was, finally given the opportunity to speak, fulfilling the call on my life, and God was having me share the words I longed to hear for myself over another woman. But the moment I read to her, something shifted inside. The lies crumbled before me. This woman was a sister, a woman of God, who had her own struggles and journey to walk in.

We met up after the retreat. I exposed my heart to this woman, owning everything. For two years, I had bought into the lie that I was disqualified because I was motivated from a pain that did not exist. A pain that was built from comparison and inferiority. All of it could have ended years ago if I had been willing to sit at the table and share my heart with her.

There were many other stories closely related to this one, and I sat down at the table with each person, exposing the lies and encountering the truth. Slowly, the lines were no longer blurry. The truth was clear. God is my qualifier, and He had a path laid out for me. I only had to surrender my plans for His.

Fast forward: married, healing from past hurts, in counseling, going to a welcoming church with a caring community, and having a family to think about—these brought me to my knees in prayer. I was reading my Bible and really listening to God.

Every moment spent with God was an encounter, and in every encounter, I felt my soul come alive. God was breathing life back into me. From the time I gave my life to God, He prepared a way.

THE LIE: I AM NOT ENOUGH

*"We have become his poetry, a re-created people that will fulfill
the destiny he has given each of us, for we are joined to Jesus,
the Anointed One. Even before we were born, God planned in
advance our destiny and the good works we would do to
fulfill it!" Ephesians 2:10*

BEFORE WE WERE MARRIED, CODY HELPED run a business in a high stakes and controversial area as a medicinal marijuana collective. God asked him to step into places where no one else would. During the first couple of years, he obtained permits and licenses that he would not otherwise have been able to because he was moving slow and methodical, and God had his hand in it.

Cody put Biblical principles into a vision statement, holding the business to an ethical standard. The business flourished and many lives were changed. For a while, I followed him to large cannabis events. Together, we ministered to the masses while being affiliated with a collective, praying over many and being a witness of the gospel in a severely greedy and lust filled environment.

Within the year, things started moving too quickly. A new man gained access to the business through a mutual connection. When this man came, things changed. To this day, I have never met him, but I had many dreams leading up to his entry into our lives.

In meeting this man, Cody was quickly pushed outside his code of ethics and running mass amounts of marijuana throughout the county and state. The money flow became massive, and it went from business to complete chaos very quickly. He was way in over his head, and I had little idea about it all.

I felt the foundation of our marriage become unsteady. Cody was coming home only a day and a half a week. This resulted in me having to choose between the kids' time or mine, ultimately ending up sacrificing our marriage.

We spent most of Sunday at church, then with the kids, and half the next day with each other before he was off to work again. The lack of quality time and intimacy caused poor connection. Without connection, we both lived our lives independently of each other. My husband made choices in our marriage I was unaware of, choices that would end up coming back around with severe consequences. The spirit of our marriage was toxic and distrustful. It triggered me, and I wanted to run.

Our therapist, Doug, was aware of everything, including my desire to leave. He responded to our session through my faith in God, asking me to continue to stay in the marriage and start interceding for my husband. I listened, and instead of pulling away, I pressed in. Every day going to war for Cody.

A corner of our house had a dining nook that I made into a prayer room. It had a seat, a desk, and a beautiful large window with a view of pastures. I spent most of my time on my knees facing that window, crying out to God for healing of our marriage. Pleading with Him for words of wisdom to say and to give me strength to say them.

I was having predictive dreams again; God came to me and showed me these very detailed and elaborate scenes of what was to come and what to do. The first dream, I was standing in a room, where there were four men Cody was working with. Three of them were behind a glass window, counting an astronomical amount of money. Cody was at a small table with a small stack of money. Suddenly, a law enforcement task force burst through the doors and arrested the three men, leaving my husband alone.

After they left, I grabbed my husband and ran to a parking lot full of cars, where we looked for a hidden bag of artifacts that would sustain our family. Hand in hand, we went from car to car, searching. In the dream, we were only able to survive if we stayed together. I woke up.

Waking up after this dream gave me the drive to be insistent with my husband, begging him to leave the workplace. This created tension in our marriage for many months, but I persisted, showing him places of deception at the workplace, sharing what God was saying to me, and praying with him consistently. The resistance continued for several more months until something finally broke.

One of the most detrimental and scariest decisions we made was getting out. Leaving required us to start completely over and would also put us in a situation that had the potential to harm us and our children. The people within the work environment had grown increasingly threatening. There was an evil spirit that was looming over, and it wanted my husband. But God wanted him more. We were obedient to His command, and He told us to get out.

In 2018, Cody met with several men, severing all attachment with the business. We were both extremely nervous and heavily weighed down about how they would handle it. He called me and told me he was breaking all ties, and to go into prayer and fasting immediately.

Soon after the phone call, when I was deeply invested in prayer, something dark and heavy entered our home. My chest was heavy and hurting. My two-year-old had a sudden fever of 106 degrees and was profusely vomiting. She was lying on the floor, and next to her was her fourteen-year-old sister, who began having a seizure. Scared, I could not understand what was happening, and was torn as to which daughter to care for first. One vomiting while the other was seizing.

Suddenly a crack began formed in the ceiling, and rain poured through. Alone and terrified, I lifted my head and cried out to God for help.

The moment I uttered Jesus' name, the fever, vomiting, seizure, and the water gushing from the ceiling abruptly ended. The phone rang. It was my husband. He said, "I did it." It was as if the veil was torn. He had chosen our marriage and been obedient to God.

When Cody came home, we began sorting out our financials and planning for a new future, one that would be surrendered to God. He wanted for our lives. But my heart was broken, because it would cost us everything we had.

Within months of the job change, a vision came to me. In it, Jesus handed me a Bible and opened it to Mark Chapter 10. He showed me things that would transpire. First, my marriage: I was going to be tested, and he pointed to verse 9:

> *So there you have it. What God has joined together, no one has*
> *the right to split apart.*

Jesus told me, "When the time comes, you will feel the need to run from your marriage because of things that were done." He said, "In that time, I want you to press into the promise of the covenant and the vows in which you shared."

Then came a vision of our kids—there were men trying to pull my husband away from our family. I was weeping and scared. He pointed to verse 14:

> *Let all the little children come to me and never hinder them!*
> *Don't you know that God's kingdom exists for such as these?*

Jesus turned toward me and said, "When the time comes, you will feel helpless and scared because it seems your family is being torn apart. Bring the children to me and know that I have them."

Finally, the last part of the vision was giving up everything. Our vehicles, our home, and everything connected to my husband's last job. In the vision, Cody was attached to everything. Jesus showed me verse 21:

> *Yet there is still one thing in you lacking. Go, sell all that you*
> *have and give the money to the poor. Then all your treasure*
> *will be in Heaven. After you've done this, come back and*
> *walk with me.*

…and after, verse 24:

Children, it is next to impossible for those who trust in their
riches to find their way into God's kingdom.

Jesus turned toward me and said, *"You will have to let go of it all for*
your husband to come back to me. Not only will you let it all go, but you will
also activate the process and begin by turning over your things first. Your new
car and your home will have to be sold."

Right away I brought the vision to my husband. I was content with
giving up all our assets, telling Cody that he was the rich young ruler,
and I wanted to believe that even if the rich young ruler had left, he did
as Jesus requested and came back to follow him.

Together, Cody and I began the quest of donating, selling, trashing,
and letting go of everything attached to his past. Giving up my dream
car first, and then selling our beautiful home. We struggled through it all
—together.

We were hopeful and terrified at the same time, making these
extremely hard decisions that would absolutely affect the family. I cried
through most of it, grieving the loss of a life we had built together. It was
a lengthy process and took some strategy, but once we started, God
blesses us with every move.

Nearly eight months after having left the business and going through
the letting go process, we received a call from a federal DEA special
agent. He was giving us a warning that they had arrested three men and
needed to talk to my husband. Like the first dream a year and a half
earlier, the task force had come in and arrested the men. The special
agent knew my husband had been out of the business, but there were
many things that he had to be accountable for.

Everything came at us fast after the phone call. We were thrown into
an active federal investigation. People from his past came to our home at
all hours, threatening us for things we did not have. I discovered choices
my husband made that were hidden from me. Things like illegal
distribution of marijuana and allowing others to use his name on bank
accounts. This led to money laundering charges.

When this came out, I was hurt. Every trust issue, lie, and misdeed
washed up on the shoreline of our marriage. What had he done? How
was I going to recover from these lies when they had put our family in a
position of significant loss? Had I known, we would have carried each

other in wisdom and strength, together as partners in marriage, enabling him to make better decisions for our family.

But God had told me this was going to happen, and so together, hand in hand, we pressed into the promises we made and worked through the pain with honesty and communication. Turning toward each other and dedicating our marriage to God, we went through forgiveness and grace without ceasing.

When the DEA presented the legal documents to us, it stated that my husband had the potential to serve a mandatory minimum of five years and a maximum of sixty in federal prison. I was afraid for our children. There was no good timing for my husband to be absent from the growth of our kids.

God reminded me of what he said: "When the time comes, you will feel helpless and scared because it seems your family is being torn apart. Bring the children to me and I know that I have them."

The strength that we were building in our marriage activated something deep within. The raging war for our family took its rightful place, and I put on the full armor of God and fought off the enemy. Nothing and no one would stand in the way of what God was doing in our lives, for our marriage, and our children. We surrendered it unto God and put all our trust in Him.

Nobody knew what we were going through, not family, friends, or church community. It was long suffering, and every Sunday at worship I would fall to my face in doubt and fear, calling out to God for answers.

There was one Sunday at church. I was sitting in the front row, and everything seemed so distant. Everyone was carrying on with normalcy, while our life felt like it was unraveling at the seams. It was too much for my heart to take. We weren't living in a normal place; we were fighting a battle for our lives and our family unit.

God showed up, and I asked him what was going to happen with my husband. He gave me two pictures, one where Cody was standing on stage and speaking to a group of people. He was free and outside the prison walls. Then he showed me a second picture...of Cody standing up in a prison suit speaking to a group of men. Two very different groups. But God said, no matter what happens to your husband, he will be ministering to my people. I cannot give you an answer to which one is true, but I need you to trust that Cody belongs to me.

It was 2019. The Lord woke me up and told me it was time to start telling our story.

From the very beginning of the legal process, we were aware of the stigma surrounding prison—the possibilities of community gossip, rejection and/or judgment. The divorce rate was well over eighty percent for families of people in the prison system. It was because of this that Cody and I decided early to listen to God's voice only throughout the process. Making moves from what our attorney advised, bringing it prayer, and answering in obedience.

When God told me to begin sharing our story, we were apprehensive, but obedient. Each week began with another person to tell, and this went on for one hundred weeks, starting with our pastors. It was difficult and intense, but their responses were filled with grace.

We called these people our *Contenders*. God cared for us through the Contenders. They fought our battles when we couldn't, encouraged us to live freedom-filled lives while they carried the pending burden. They protected us from gossip, supported us through rejection and judgment. With their help, we told others with increasing confidence and ease, releasing the stigma of it all.

The Contenders made it possible through face-to-floor prayer, fasting, and communion as we continued to strive for hope.

Amazingly, we discovered joy in the suffering. The joy we experienced did not devalue the grief in the difficult times, but our deep faith in God responded with laughter through pain and hope in the process.

Every day since our family's decision to walk in obedience, we have had to say goodbye to something of great value. When it felt like we had nothing more to give and we were losing all we had, we would turn to Jesus and walk back into the freedom he promised us.

The Lord graciously reminded us we have never been in want, and looking back, there have been many victories.

In 2020, the time came for my husband to plea before a judge.

I lost it, running toward fear with open arms. Keeping it to myself, an internal rage built and opened a door to the lie that I was not enough. The enemy got full access to my runaway thoughts, bitter with my husband for receiving support while he was the one who had made poor choices. All while I had to sit alone, in the background, suffering the potential pain that lie ahead of us and the kids.

Being not enough became fear. Fear of our kids being raised alone, fear of losing hard-built memories, fear of our daughter dying from a seizure, fear of losing my kids. The fear became all things past, present, and future, a convoluted scene of lies, creating a million non-existing scenes of what-ifs.

The hopes and dreams of a beautiful marriage and family seemed to slip away. My husband was the absolute love of my life, and I felt like I was going to lose him.

Despite the fears, the anxiety, and all the lies, I turned toward Jesus and closed my eyes. Feeling his comforting warm arms wrap around me, I cried. We stayed there together for a long while until he woke me out of my slumber with a sweet reminder that I was enough for all these things and much more. While I lay there in peace and assurance, I wondered out loud, how did Paul find joy in prison?

When the court date arrived. In just a few short minutes, he would be approaching a federal judge and making a plea of guilt with the possibility of time in prison.

Prison, the term that brought us to our knees. A word that would constantly bring sorrow, shame, and so much pain. I watched as my husband was getting ready, trying to pull strength out of myself and be the wife God called me to be.

My husband turned and asked me to adjust his tie. I wiggled the fabric into place and realized he was wearing the tie from our wedding day. As a tear ran down my cheek, he leaned over and kissed me. Everything that was supposed to separate us instead pressed us together in a love that never fails, a love strong as death, and a love that was enough.

11

THE LIE: I AM TOO MUCH

"But when you yield to a life of the Spirit, you will no longer be living under the law, but soaring above it!" Galatians 5:18

WITH MUCH ENCOURAGEMENT AND PRAYER, Cody joined Emerge Discipleship Intensive. Men surrounded him, empowering him as he confronted hard places in his life. And in those places, he grew.

We came to realize if we were not going through all the legal battles, there would not have been the exponential growth we needed for our marriage and family. Being confronted with a lingering and painful "what-if," and being able to say that it was a blessing, is exactly why we are where we are today.

There was an understanding that the judicial system outside of God was one designed to perpetuate shame. Upon release from prison, you carry a record that reminds you of a past, one that can and will create hardships. Often we hear prisoners are no longer considered productive citizens.

Cody and I waged war against these statements by remaining open and honest about everything in our lives, flipping the script and stigma on what society was saying about flawed people, to what God says about us. God sent his only son to deliver us from a past of shame and sin. He paid our debt, and we have been forgiven through his death at the cross.

To this day, Cody has not been sentenced. We continue to sit in the waiting on whether he goes to prison. If or when the time comes to stand before a judge, we both know my husband's repentant heart will prevail over the gavel that deems him guilty. However, the testimony is not in the result, but how we got through it all with strength, obedience, and faith.

Together we rejoice in our freedom through salvation, one not dependent on whether Cody gains freedom through a judge.

When my husband completed his Emerge year, he came home with a beautiful and intense story of how God encountered him, his heart pressed for our covenant and what God had in store for us both.

He woke me out of a sleep in the early morning with a gift. Gently lifting me up and seating me on the edge of the bed, he knelt on one knee just below my dangling feet. He had placed a large bowl full of water on the floor.

My husband's long hair flowed around his shoulders, and through my blurry morning eyes appeared as an image of Jesus. Pulling out a towel and placing it on his knee, with great tenderness, he lifted the back of my leg, ran his hand down to my foot, and placed it gently into the bowl of water.

The history of washing feet is significant of servanthood. Jesus turned a slave-like act into a deeply loving and spiritual cleansing. I imagined myself in the room; it stole my breath away. Giving me indication that my Savior was about to move in an act of servanthood. He pours water into the basin, lifts Peter's dirty feet, and washes them.

Putting myself in Peter's place, I imagine he stops Jesus because of pride, confusion, and angst. Jesus answers Peter.

> *"If you don't allow me to wash your feet, then you will not be able to share life with me."*

My husband washed my feet.

I cried with extravagant love as my husband apologized for every affliction that had burdened my soul from past relationships, including himself. Then he dried my feet, and with every wipe he prayed a new prayer and promise into my life.

From my hands to my feet, brokenness to healing, forfeit to victory, destruction to salvation, the washing of my feet was a supernatural cleansing of the deep love in our covenant through an obedient act of a husband washing the feet of his wife.

God showed me that our marriage is fortified through communion, taking the traditional idea of marriage—something ordinary to society— and turning it into a kingdom celebration by becoming uniquely intimate and profound within His design for our marriage journey.

The closest thing we will experience to Heaven is carrying out our marriage, breaking off generational pains, and bringing in a newfound legacy of power through His love.

In the book of John, Chapter 2, Jesus attended a wedding. The wine was running low, and his mother sent for him to provide more. There were six stoneware water pots. The Jews used these pots for ritual washing of purification, and they were usually about twenty to thirty gallons. It was pertinent that no person defile the pots, keeping them pure. Jesus commanded the servants fill the pots with water and, in a miracle, the water became wine for the wedding party. The pots of purification had turned into a sacrament of celebration, a holy communion at a wedding.

Then, in Luke, Chapter 22, Jesus is sitting at the table with his disciples, enjoying the Passover meal. He lifts his cup, blesses it, and asks it to be passed around, saying, *"This cup is the new covenant written in my blood, blood poured out for you."*

Jesus died after Passover, a covenant of sacrament for our lives. From the first miracle at the wedding to the last at the cross, Jesus showed the way through communion and covenant. And from this, He has shown Cody and me what covenant truly looks like.

Together, we stepped into the promise of freedom in our lives, expressed in action through the vows we made to each other on the day we were married.

Both of us experienced encounters with God, and in those encounters, we rose into the unique and authentic purpose over our lives. One that called out to live unapologetically in Christ and in the gifts we experienced in the Holy Spirit.

With an uncontained fire raging deep within our souls, my husband and I became an active part of the Emerge ministry and leadership team around 2019.

I was not raised in a charismatic church, so when I began experiencing encounters with the Holy Spirit, I automatically retreated to an unseen place. God continued to call me up and out of those places, but the voices of others would rise above the voice of God, telling me to tone it down or that I was too much.

Often when I would receive a word of wisdom, a vision of something that may transpire, or a dream of what God was doing, I would become so emotional that it would create tension in the room. On a couple of occasions, I was asked to not practice my gifts. I was making people feel uncomfortable.

I was told to tone down the emotional presentation when delivering the message, because I was crying a lot. I was referred to as the weeping prophet Jeremiah. Jeremiah was a grieved prophet for his people, and he expressed it through tears and suffering. He felt the burden of what was to come for them. But it was his cross to bear out of obedience to God, and he continued in it with much courage.

I had a deep understanding of this prophet, whom I love to call "the passionate prophet" instead of a weeper. Passionate in emotion for what he felt and knew. But, in the end, Jeremiah delivered a message of hope. And just as I delivered a message from God to a group of people, there was always someone restored in hope.

When moved by the Spirit, it would agitate, provoke, and then stir something deep within. If God wanted me to deliver a message, the person on the receiving end was always ready for it. It was the rest of the room that became uncomfortable. But God knew all of this.

There was a constant push and pull: being obedient in Christ versus the honor of my peers. The gifts in me felt too outrageous to some, causing tension and irritation. Occasionally, people asked me to leave in an attempt to silence the Spirit within me. I couldn't understand why the Holy Spirit was so offensive to some people.

While I was moved by my gifts through the Spirit, those gifts simultaneously moved my emotions. We are made in God's image, that includes all the emotions we have been given to experience when partnered with the Spirit.

I wept at what I saw, and for what would happen with every

compassionate movement of God in and through His people. For those who knew, and for those who did not *yet* know the goodness of Jesus. Being angry for the injustices and waging war through prayer. Leaping and dancing with praise at every testimony of faithfulness.

With every confident and unfettered move Cody and I made, the enemy attempted to make demands on our lives. When we ignored those demands, he used the public to stop to us. Hearing words like, *you are too much,* or *you are intimidating.* Finding myself enriched by salvation, but becoming steadily complacent in obedience because of what others thought of me.

Despite being grieved at the isolating tension of having people see us as something other than disciples of Christ, every emotion increased my confidence. Confidence to walk in obedience of God's voice. Confidence to lead in a bold and compassionate way that cared for the hearts of others. I was passionate for His people.

Our growth, the loyalty in friendships, and respect for our leadership was unmatched. A family of people had loved us to the frontline for battle. But I was not equipped with the full armor of God, wearing everything except the "belt of truth." I was layered in lies, the last of which was being *too much* for the confines of the corporate church community. We felt caught between dishonor of our peers or the disobedience of God.

Through it all, Cody and I kept moving, journeying through the gospel, surrendering ourselves in worship, and deepening our prayer life with our face to the floor. There was no turning back.

With my past work experience in psychiatry and crisis intervention, my life experiences, and a growing relationship with God, we decided to build a ministry in trauma informed care. A place where people could come and learn tools and exercises to help them sustain a life after trauma.

With that experience, I was able to guide others through breaking off old patterns, shifting views and responses, and help them obtain a confident and authentic life through hardships, grief, adversity, and trauma.

It was successful, but while many were thriving after their journey through the curriculum, I was becoming increasingly unhealthy. Suffering through heightened obsessive-compulsive disorder and post-traumatic stress. [1]

I was hiding everything from everyone, fearing that leadership would fault me as incapable. The irony of it all was that hiding it created my own incapability. The lies over the years had piled on so heavily that the weight was making great attempts to destroy all we built.

It was too much, and I remember uttering the disgusted words, "I am too much for them and not good enough for you God!" Sickened with grief, I took a posture of surrender. And every Sunday for a year, during worship, I laid it down—my life, my marriage, and my children—at the foot of the cross.

12

NO MORE LIES!

"But I promise you this, the Holy Spirit will come upon you, and you will be seized with power." Acts 1:8

IN JANUARY OF 2020, MY HUSBAND AND I WERE POWERING THROUGH THE legal battles with mighty faith. We were listening with obedient intent, each step of our life choices belonging only to God and what He wanted for us, while honoring the leaders of Emerge in their ministry. Cody was a mentor with a group of young men, and I was coming alongside the creative team with a vision for what God wanted in each season of new people. Together, we interceded over the students of Emerge, laying on hands and speaking truth and wisdom into the depths of their heart.

We were a team. Powerful in the Spirit, and fluid in the mighty movement of God. We worshipped together, unfettered and with abandon, reading the Bible daily and taking its breath to battle. We were called to the people, and we were called in it together.

Our bond was unbreakable, and with the looming possibility of my husband going to prison, we chose each other above all things. It was the mandate of our lives, often hearing that we were "the power couple." We had our team of Contenders praying over us daily, surrounding us with support and much favor.

Each year, the Emerge team has a Deeper Life Retreat, a three-day event tucked away in a beautiful little forest grove in Chico, California. Every year is unique to the students, the lead team, and what God has planned. There are several areas to go walk and hike, get some alone time with God, and retreat into a still place.

There are three main trails. One leads you toward a beautiful pool of water formed inside a rocky creek above a cascading waterfall. Another trail winds along pastures and up the mountainside toward three perfectly placed crosses. The third—the main one—runs up terrain near a steep hillside that rises above the entire grove.

The first year my husband and I went together, we made the journey up the terrain with lumber, nails, and a hammer. This was no easy task; I am so afraid of heights, it can be debilitating. But he was patient with me as he guided me along the steep slopes and while I worked through my fears.

When we reached the top, we built the cross. On our knees, we dug a hole with our bare hands. Steadily, we placed the cross into the hole and stacked rocks all around. The moment we planted the cross, God began speaking holy promises of love and truth over us, sharing His sweetness of favor as we continued walking in obedience.

From the time we left the campus, and for the entire rest of that year, God showed up with answered prayers. We often cried with so much gratitude and hope. Our love abounded.

The following year, 2021, it was once again time for Deeper Life Retreat. Cody and I were deeply invested and looked forward to meeting God in the same place to solidify what the year had brought to us.

However, for this retreat, they had limited finances and available spaces. Only Cody was going to be able to attend. The odds were stacking against us at a rapid rate. For days, we struggled through the idea that we may not be able to go together. In honor of our marriage, he was prepared to stay home. Through tears and pain, we knew saying no to his mentees would be difficult. But our choice to stay together was an obedient one, and in that my husband would share with the young men that a marriage comes first before ministry.

Yet we believed it was God's will over our marriage to stand strong together as a team and in His will. We began to pray. If God had something in store for us, He would provide a way.

Within 48 hours of going to prayer, we received a call, asking both of us to attend the Deeper Life Retreat. The blessing of obedience was abundantly clear.

The theme for the year was from the book of Ezekiel, about speaking life into our dry bones. We would learn that God's power and plan for us surpasses all the limitations we have put on ourselves by making us new again.

My husband and I were tasked with collecting bones during the month leading up to the retreat. A strange request, but the bones part of a creative scene to bring the book of Ezekiel to life. About a week prior to us leaving, my husband heard God say there would be bones at the retreat site. We showed up a day early with an intentional plan of bone hunting.

Setting out with purpose, we carried a backpack containing juice and bread for communion and walked upstream for the one mile hike to the top of the cascading waterfall. A natural pool formed at the top, almost like a baptismal, and we sat down and shared communion together.

Our prayers filled the air, praying for every person coming into the weekend. We prayed with expectancy for breakthrough and deliverance. Both my husband and I surrendering all of us right there at the pool, our hearts filled with the overflowing of the Holy Spirit. My husband got up and took a plunge into the ice-cold pool. He popped out of the water, stood up, and yelled loudly, "COME ALIVE!"

His voice echoing through the ravine, he cried out three more times.

And then there was complete silence. In the stillness, God said, "A miracle is about to happen."

Not far off was a friend of ours, and when he heard my husband cry out, the Lord prompted him to turn around and come to us. He stood on a rock a few feet away with a look of wonder on his face. I called him over, gave him communion, and all three of us ventured out looking for bones.

We crossed the pasture on a small trail just below the crosses. I was doubtful we would find bones in an open pasture, so I postured myself in a space of silent prayer, giving gratitude for the vastness of God's surrounding work.

Once we hit the tree line, the three of us split up to cover more ground, yelling out occasionally, asking if anyone had found a bone. My husband had not given up on it yet.

He roared, "God, rattle the bones that we might find them and hear them!"

Seconds after Cody yelled out, we heard our friend behind us. "I found a bone!"

My husband evoked the Spirit according to scripture, and the bones kept popping up. It was surreal, a movement of great faith, and with it we leapt with joy and laughter.

Cody asked our friend, "Have you found a carcass?" "No."

And with that, my husband roared out one last time. "Lord! Rattle the bones!"

And just like before, we were standing right near a carcass of bones, all of us screaming with excitement, in awe of the glory in which we were experiencing.

God had revealed bones to the prophet Ezekiel. He stood among a valley of dry bones, just as we stood, surrounded by bones, bones rattled up by the prayers of my husband. Imagining the prophet standing there with as much emotion as I was—nervous and unsure, but filled with reverence and hope.

In the book of Ezekiel, people were in exile. This is how my life felt for so very long, exiled and detached, working from a place of constant trauma. It was time to come out of exile, and that scared me. But I knew there was a pivotal shift happening in my life, answers to long awaited prayers, and God had more for me on the horizon.

The Lord quietly whispered, "It is time to go. Leave the men here."

NO MORE LIES! 103

They were still finding bones as their delightful screams faded in the distance during my trek back to the campus. God and I continued talking about the prophet in Ezekiel. After the prophet was led to the dry bones, he was asked to revitalize them back to life through prophecy and prayer. All the bones of hopelessness received the spirit of resurrection through the commanding breath of God's name.

*"Our new faith in Jesus transfers God's righteousness to us and
he now declares us flawless in his eyes. This means we can
now enjoy true and everlasting peace with God, all because of
what our Lord Jesus, the Anointed One, has done for us"*
Romans 5:1

That evening, I stepped into worship. The space was dim, and from the door to the front of the room there was a stunning, long pathway of vibrant green foliage. A multitude of candles illuminated fresh spring flowers. Walking along the green pathway toward the music, you could see deep within the foliage where the brightly colored flowers were tucked inside all the dry bones we collected on our miraculous walk that day.

We received instructions to follow in the footsteps of the prophet Ezekiel. The bones represented all the dead things in our lives, from anxiety to hopelessness. Anything in your life that was keeping you dead. We were to pick up a bone and declare all things new in the mighty name of the Lord.

There I stood, staring at the bones, struggling with every hopeless and slain part of me to pick up a bone. Through tearful eyes, I saw others around me picking up their own dry bones. Each person called out to our sovereign Lord for their life to awaken. They were bold and brave. I wasn't. Comparison relentlessly pursued my thoughts.

Sick to my stomach, the war between restoration and atrophy overwhelmed me. My husband showed up with a bone in his hand—he wanted us to do this together as a symbol of bringing our marriage back to life. Triggered, I missed his intent and fell into his chest. He comforted me with encouraging words and a prayer, then excused himself to pray over the others in the room.

Left standing there with a bone in my hand, I locked eyes with my friend Mary. She was a place of safety and care. The understanding she carried was a gift, and it was enough for me to break from my paralytic state. I moved across the room to her and we left for a private room.

We sat at a small table with couches on either side, the room still and peaceful. I shared with her my deepest fears—the struggle with post-traumatic stress disorder, and how triggered I was having to go through the process of bringing myself back to life.

The moment at the table with Mary stirred me to want a better outcome, a real transformation. She was prayerful and full of wisdom, encouraging me through stories of her own life. But I still had so many questions, so much I was not ready to let go of, and this angered me. In the anger, I grabbed the bone off the table, ran back into the decorated room, and threw the bone back into the foliage.

I went to bed that night exhausted and discouraged.

I woke the next morning faced with new challenges, frustrated for not vocalizing the constant painful and ever-growing dialogue I struggled with. I had spent the last year surrendering my life to God and walking in obedience by inspiring the life of trauma survivors. But I still could not grasp my own inner healing, stuck in literal chaos.

Yet God was not giving up on me. He was speaking to my friend and pastor of Emerge, Jim Bailey. Jim was a constant in my life. He baptized me in 2014, married us in 2015, and dedicated our daughter in 2016. Jim invested in our family, and I loved both him and his wife, Amy, who had been my Emerge mentor. But loving someone and trusting them were two wildly different things.

Jim had gotten wind that I skipped out the night before, and when I came into worship the next morning, he pulled me up in front of the room. Placing two bones in my hands, he told the students that leaders were not without their own journey. But as leaders, we would lead the way.

Jim set the tone for bravery, making space for God to show up. The idea that leaders had to have their lives completely together as a well-rounded, perfect Christian was a lie, and it was tested the moment he laid those bones in my hands.

I stood there in the brightly lit room, nowhere to hide, in front of people who did not know the real me and all I had been through. They were staring at the open book Rita, the one who wore her heart on her sleeve, and Renee, the one who had many deep internal and painful secrets.

When I flew to Redding and started my life over, I adopted the name Rita, my maternal grandmother's name. Grandmother Rita was not spoken of often. When she died, so did the conversations about her. It was a tragic loss and very painful for the family, so they called me by my second name, Renee, meaning born again.

Rita meant pearl. A pearl forms when an irritant becomes trapped inside an oyster's shell and it secretes its own protection agent. Together, the process of protection and the irritant produce a perfect formation—the pearl. The pearl becomes most valuable the longer the irritant stays, taking months or sometimes years.

Hiding behind the name Rita for eleven years was just like the formation of a pearl. I spent years shaping and molding myself, becoming a new story. This was me in my shell. Holy Spirit came in like a wave, bringing a tiny grit of sand with it. My own self-protective measures were nothing against the Spirit. I was not ready to let go, but the irritant was becoming too much. Rita, standing with two bones in my hands, feeling faint and extremely vulnerable.

The admittance of my past and who I really was underneath the cover was too much. I faced exposure. My pulse raced, my mind went into automatic flight mode, I triggered, anxiety rose to the forefront. Death felt nearby, circling the room, wanting me to hide behind the multitude of lies I had built. My head hung down like a huge heavy burden, afraid to look it in the eye.

God whispered, "look up." With everything I had in me, I lifted my head to face it all. At first glance, I saw my husband. Smiling proudly, his sweet safety giving me just enough hope to look to the next person, Jim, and the next, Kim, Betty, Billy, Matt. One by one, God showed up in each person's face, in those people I had grown to trust. My breathing slowed, my heart rate steadied. Death left, and grace flooded the room.

Holy Spirit was the time keeper, expanding the minutes until I was able to speak, and when I did, I yelled it all out. Years of trauma spewing out of me like foreign objects that had bound me and diseased me sick. "The assault! The abuse! My body! Stolen peace!" I kept going until there was a release, then silence. It created a void that cried out to the Lord, "Fill it back up!" "Truth, hope, and peace."

Like the prophet Ezekiel, I was prophesying and praying the spirit of resurrection over my life through the commands of God, through scripture and truth. Jim anointed my hands with a prayer oil, and then with a kind voice directed me to walk out into the wilderness and bury the victim part of me—calling out the young girl that was forgotten so long ago, and walk with her in silence for the entire day.

I left the room thinking it was all over; the work had been done and it was time to revere it all. But God was far from done with me. He wanted more than breakthrough; God wanted deliverance.

"At last we have freedom, for Christ has set us free! We must always cherish this truth and firmly refuse to go back into the bondage of our past" Galatians 5:1

I walked into the adjoining room first, a beautiful prayer space set up with flowy white curtains, dim lighting, and soft sounds of water fountains filling the air. There were prayer stations, uniquely designed so each person would have a internal discovery through a prayer-filled and creative process.

One station stood out to me; my friend Glory had set it up. It was a clay and pottery table, with instruction on forming our own unique piece of clay, having in mind how God formed us. There was scripture to guide us into a deep and methodical process. Holding the clay in my hands—wet, smooth, and smelling like earth—I asked God to reveal my formation. He said, *"You were formed from the dust of the ground, but it was my breath that gave you life."*

I wrote a list of all the things in me that needed to come back to life. The enemy had made many attempts on my life over the years, trying with all his might to suck the very breath back out of me through lies. Lies I wore and lies placed on me, woven tightly around my very existence like a boa constrictor squeezing its prey. The enemy wants us all to turn away from God, but a person who has authority and power in Christ—that person, the enemy wants dead.

I warmed the piece of clay in my hands until I was able to smooth it flat on the table. Then, gently and strategically, I placed each piece of paper on it. Written with words of life and truth, I pressed them firmly into the clay, shaping and molding it as a symbol of my life. I set it into my bag along with a Bible, journal, and a pen, then I left for the wilderness to which God was calling me.

I followed the trail up the incline toward the cross my husband I built a year ago on the highest part of the mountain. At the top there was a giant rock with a hole which opened to a trail running along a very narrow, steep path along the side of the mountain.

Just as I came out of the rock and stepped onto the steep terrain, I froze. I have always been terrified of high places, and with nothing to hold on to except the side of a rocky mountain, fear gripped me. I sank into a crouch and scurried my backside up against the rocks as tight as I could. My husband was not there to guide me this time. I sat there with my toes nearing the edge, with no one to help, so I prayed.

After a while, I became aware I could be stuck out there all night. I found the strength to scoot my butt along the edge without getting up, little by little, until a young man came around the corner. He was an Emerge student.

This young man was hiking when he realized he had lost his water bottle. God told him to go back and look for it. To his surprise, he found me scooting along the trail. Breaking silence, I asked for help. Without a single word, he reached his hand out to me, lifted me up, and guided me off the steep terrain.

I cried when he left. People had hurt me for so long, and it caused trust issues—*especially* with men. As a result, I had become very self-sufficient and strong willed. God sent this young man to me, guiding me out of danger, and I had to trust him. There was gentleness in his hands, a grace for what I was going through. It had been a long time since I trusted a man I did not know.

When I reached the top of the mountain, the cross Cody and I built was gone. There was nothing but a stack of rocks in its place. Stacked stones were significant. In the Bible, stones were used as markers, claiming a space of land. Boundary markers to keep people out unless there was permission to reap from the land. People also used stones as a memorial or reminder. In the book of Joshua, he led the twelve tribes of Israel into the Promised Land. He told each tribe to carry a stone out of the river and build an altar as a reminder to the people that God led them safely on their journey.

Both stories were symbolically true for me. Even though the cross was not there, the stones represented our marriage—setting boundary, staking claim, a holy reminder of the journey to safety we had been on together. Taking each stone off and setting it to the side, I dug a hole in the dirt beneath their base. The clay formation out of my bag fit perfectly in the shallow grave. I piled the dirt and stones back on top in a ceremonial fashion.

A single tree stood nearby. I walked over to it and laid myself under its shade. Closing my eyes, I was brought into a dream. It was the story of Elijah. In 1 Kings, it describes a story of a man who had been exposed, and was scared. In fear, he ran into the desert when he came to a lone tree. Elijah collapsed under the tree, begging God for his death. He fell asleep, but an angel woke him with food and water for nourishment. The story continues until God visits Elijah on top of a mountain in a way he had not experienced: a quiet and gentle whisper.

Suddenly, in place of Elijah, it was me. God whispered, "Rise up, daughter." I got up and out from under the shelter of the tree and tried to leave, but was afraid of leaving behind all had I buried under the stones. I walked over to edge of the cliff where the stones lay.

Nourished, obedient, I waited on his voice for hope after the breakthrough of the morning. I let out a lengthy sigh and God spoke again, "RISE UP! You are no longer in exile!" Then a gust of wind came rushing off the side of the cliff, hit the stones, and brushed my face, as if God was breathing me back to life from the very clay I buried.

Stepping back, I tried to leave once again. Fear kept pulling me back in. I did not know who I was outside the deepest moments of suffering, without trauma. My identity had become it all, convoluted with lies, and the truth felt distant. God spoke a third time. "RISE UP! COME ALIVE YOU WARRIOR!"

Continuing to ignore the voice, I tried to leave again. Starting out along the second trail across the field and down the back side of the mountain, stopping as I was about to lose sight of the stones. Afraid of who I was going to be, how I was going to navigate through life without it all. I believed myself to be all the things I had gone through. I turned toward the stones, wanting to dig the clay form back up again.

Just as I reached the stones, God spoke with such fierceness that my entire body fell back. His anger was kindled on my behalf:

"You have held on to lies for far too long. It says, I am the Way and the Truth and the Life. You are a new person in me. Your name will go back to Renee, meaning born again. You will grow with her from where she was left. I will restore the memories that the moments of trauma covered up for so long, flooding your soul with truth. You will no longer minister from a place of experience, those places kept alive with every spoken word. You will listen to my Wisdom, and I will guide you all your days. Leave here with a new heart and a new life. One that your children and grandchildren will reap the harvest of."

His voice went silent, the wind died, and a warm sensation began flowing through my blood. The presence of God was so tangible that I was unable to contain myself and began laughing uncontrollably. So much joy! I sat there on my knees in the dirt, with my hands covering my face, laughing.

I ran back down the trail, unrestrained in newfound freedom, back to the retreat. Through the door, I saw Jim. I ran to him, broke my silence, and told him it was time for me to rededicate my life to Jesus. He simply pointed to the cross sitting in the middle of the room.

That day, I laid at the foot of the cross, weeping, and invited Jesus back into my newly restored heart.

Jesus answered, "I speak an eternal truth: Unless you are born of water and the Spirit, you will never enter God's kingdom."
John 3:5

The next day, the last day of retreat, I woke up exhausted from all that had taken place over the weekend, but still revitalized in Christ and ready for morning worship.

While standing in the back and swaying in the music, I asked God to take me back to the twelve-year-old girl I was before there was pain. Wanting to care for her vulnerability and pray for her sweet safety. Transformation happened this weekend, raw breakthrough, and I thanked the Lord for renewed memories and a clean heart.

There were many in this room full of people who were struggling with so much of the same thing. One woman, a student at this Deeper Life Retreat, was relentless in her pursuit of breakthrough. She was gifted in worship, and was invited up front to sing her way out of pain. Her powerful voice drew the presence of the Holy Spirit into the room. I climbed onto a chair in the back so I could get a clearer view.

My hands lifted into the air, receiving all His grace and mercy, praying,

"I release the identity of trauma to you, Lord, accepting my identity in you and living out my life obedient to your voice. Lord, release me of anxiety, depression, post-traumatic stress, and obsessive behaviors! I surrender all my ways and make them your own."

On that chair, soaking in the goodness of His love, I heard the woman switch to her native tongue. She was singing in Swahili. Ever since I was a little girl, God gave me dreams of Africa. Over the years, He nurtured my love for it through friends and connections, so it holds a very special place in my heart.

When she sang in Swahili, God knew it would move me. My heart stirring with her angelic tone, I moved toward the front and bowed before God in holy surrender. A deep reverence welled up and washed over me and I sobbed without ceasing.

Jim came over and put his hand on my forehead. He prayed for me... healing words, full of compassion and safety. A surge of warmth rushed through me as women gathered all around, holding and rocking me. I felt blankets and fabric flowing around my body, and some of the women were petting my hair. Kindness overflowed.

Jesus showed up; I felt his warmth. His presence was so tangible as he reached forward and touched me, my soul crying out loud with the tenderness. He touched every molecular part of my DNA, expelling anything that did not belong there. I felt something come out of me, a mayhem of emotion and pain. I screamed out. My soul alternated between life and death, waling in celebration and shrieking in anger, the enemy waging war as God's love moved in.

At that moment, I became acutely aware of what Mary felt when she surrendered herself and every demon that plagued her, at the foot of Jesus. Carrying the identity that the people placed on her as well as her own doing. I sensed the depths of her cries as she washed his hair.

A woman next to me began speaking in tongues, but I could understand what she was saying. She was crying out the truth over my life, saying things that only I would know. My body came fully alive, on fire as my husband in the background yelling out:

"Get her, God! Bring her home! Come Alive, my wife! For her kids, Lord!"

My soul crying out with every ounce of tenderness I felt, God's love raining kindness on me. Then suddenly, there was peace. I sat up, felt the release. I knew without doubt that God had just cured me of PTSD. This was not something I had experienced in my lifetime. What had just happened was not another breakthrough or transformation. It was deliverance. Just when I thought God had healed me from my past, there was more. With every obedient act in His voice, I was blessed with more of Him.

Within moments of all this happening, our group moved outside to a small creek that ran through the retreat site. People were standing up above the rocks and all along the bank. One by one, each person entered the water, while others cried out with worship and prayer—yelling words of wisdom and singing praise.

Many of the leaders were in the water, surrounding each person who entered. My husband was stirring the water with such intensity, interceding for deliverance. The presence of the Holy Spirit was breathtaking. I had my camera, through tears capturing every moment —each person going under and coming up out of the water with a transformation that was so evident. And with each transformation, the Lord whispered to me, "Your turn."

After the last person had gone in, Jim turned toward me and asked me out and into the water. All my support system surrounded me, people who were not afraid of my mess, never leaving, even if I had tried pushing them away. The loyalty encompassing me in that moment was the safest I ever felt in a community of people.

Jim had baptized me years before at the Stirring, but not in the capacity in which God had me this day: Rededicating my life to the Lord, delivered from my past, and on the healing journey of a lifetime. Standing in the cool river, ready to be washed in the Spirit. I lifted my face toward Heaven.

Spending most of my life controlling the narrative, allowing others to take the reins, had spun me completely out of control. And believing in God and praying to Him had not been enough to derail the enemy's attempts to take me out. I had to trust—completely die to myself, come out in faith that God had a plan for me.

Head up, I opened my eyes and stared directly into the most beautiful bright sunbeam I had ever seen. I yelled out, "God! Immerse me into the unknown with you!" And then, with one swift movement, I went under.

I surged up out of the water, born again, whispering my given name: *Renee.*

My husband and my supporting friends were right there, holding me tight and praying over me as the very last of my fears fell away with every drop of water. God laid a patchwork blanket on my shoulders, each piece carrying the fruit of the Spirit: joy that overflows, peace that subdues, patience that endures, kindness in action, a life full of virtue, faith that prevails, gentleness of heart, and strength of Spirit.

Beloved is who I am, and there is no *thing*—trauma, addiction, pain, or choice—he can't undo. Walking out of the water that day felt more real than any traumatic event I had endured. The warrior side of me, the part of me that God designed, had been buried by layers of lies and pain.

Underneath it all, a young girl was buried, forgotten. She carried the memories full of amazing adventures, laughter, family, and friends. She carried the dreams of a life with God, the call on her life. Her name is Renee, meaning born again, and she came back to life the moment she rose up out of her grave!

It says in John, Chapter 8,

"For if you embrace the truth, it will release true freedom into your lives."

And this is my mandate to walk out as a living testimony, sharing it with all who cross my path.

WALKING IN TRUTH

YOUR OWN JOURNEY

I HAVE LEFT THE LIE AND AM NOW IN THE JOURNEY OF WALKING IN TRUTH. WE ALL HAVE OUR OWN UNIQUE JOURNEY IN CHRIST TO WALK OUT.

AND SO, INSTEAD OF SHARING THE STORY OF MY TRUTH AND THE REVELATION I WALK IN, I WANT TO EXTEND TO YOU YOUR OWN PERSONAL DEVOTIONAL BY GUIDING YOU THROUGH WHAT GOD HAS REVEALED.

WELCOME TO YOUR OWN TRUTH JOURNEY!

1

THE FIRST BRAVE STEP

"In their hearts, humans plan their course, but the Lord establishes their steps." Psalm 16:9

The first brave step is forgiveness

"Therefore, each one must answer for himself and give a personal account of his own life before God." Romans 14:12

Pain and suffering were never the end of you, they were the beginning. The beginning of a freedom that works for you and not against you, pressing and driving you toward the truth.

We can blame it all on our suffering, allowing trauma to be the thing that holds us back. Continuing to scream out obscenities, fighting a battle of lies that said we were caged in by the inflictions on us. Or we can take responsibility.

The moment we succumb to trauma, we put ourselves in a caged environment. Once we have entered the cage, everything that happens after, is our own doing. We cannot be caged without some level of compliance because we were set free the moment God sent His only son to die for us.

Responsibility to forgive is our freedom, it allows you to run wild and childlike in exactly who God created you to be. Taking your eyes off yourself and the circumstances of your yesterdays and fixating on who God says you are.

Being forgiving for something that happened to you, without choice or at the hands of another, is a process that is very difficult and sometimes people are unwilling to go through.

Healing and forgiveness cannot happen outside of God. You will find your entire life built around revenge.

Unforgiveness

"The God of passionate love will meet with me. My God will empower me to rise in triumph over my foes." Psalm 59:10

Trauma can be a long walk through the valley of pain and ending up at a fork in the road. You have two paths to choose leading to the same steep mountain.

One path is unforgiveness it looks easy and short but what you can't see is all the rocky terrain that lie ahead. The other path is forgiveness, it looks harder at a glance but what you cannot see, is how beautiful it is, with flowers and manicured trail.

Choosing the path of unforgiveness because it looks easier, is choosing the most difficult journey. You will pick up offenses along the way, and with every offense comes bitterness and anger. Every step along the rocky and offensive terrain you are gaining blisters, bruises, and your body breaks down. Blaming all the added and unnecessary pain on everyone else even though you chose the path.

I was healed and ready to take on life, but had one more thing to say, a battle to fight for all the injustices done. The injustices that caused anxiety, panic attacks and nightmares I endured for years at the hand of the offender. The fear lived in, from the manipulation and control over my life.

I walked on the pathway of unforgiveness, toward the steep mountain, in a climb toward revenge. I was ready to lash out at every offender or perpetrator in your life, pointing my finger at every person who hurt me and yell from the top of the mountain all the abuse, wounded words, deep afflictions that had impeded on my life.

Finally making it to the top, after years of journey, weak, wounded, and filled with revenge. I was ready to fight, face to face with the offender. But at the top of this mountain was not a place of retaliation and the offender was not there.

I came face to face with God. Just the two of us up there, He says to me, "are you ready to let it all go, starting with yourself first. Living in unforgiveness is keeping the offender an idol over your life. No idols come before me."

Forgiving yourself

> "For I know the thoughts that I think toward you, says the Lord, thoughts of peace and not of evil, to give you a future and a hope." Jeremiah 29:11 (KJV)

This is the part where I wish I had all the answers. I wish could tell you what it looks like to begin the process of forgiving oneself, I can tell you it is not easy.

Forgiving yourself is an individual journey between you and God and very individualized journey according to each person and what they must walk through.

Acknowledging the fact that some of the pain you feel is because of choices you made and being accountable for the part you played in that pain, is the hardest thing you will have to journey through.

Nobody wants to admit that they allowed the offender to keep them victimized, or, rationalizing unforgiveness allowed more painful things in at your own will.

Experiencing the pain all over again when God bring to surface the offense that needs forgiveness. This time, there will be nobody there to blame. It is a face-to-face time with God and yourself, sorting through it all.

Forgiving yourself is easier when there is nobody assigned the blame

> *"And everything I've taught you is so that the peace which is in me will be in you and will give you great confidence as you rest in me. For in this unbelieving world, you will experience trouble and sorrows, but you must be courageous, for I have conquered the world!" John 16:33*

It may never have been your fault, just like most wounds, it can be at the hands of someone else. What if, it was just you and a friend of yours standing in your home. You get into a heated argument. It has been a toxic friendship for a while and the tension is at an all-time high, the friend is angry and grabs a knife, stabbing at you and slicing open your arm, seriously wounding you. You are bleeding and need immediate medical attention.

Immediately going into defense mode and try to save yourself, you would grab a rag throwing it on the wound and call emergency, simultaneously kicking them out of our home. It is an automatic response to care for ourselves and then call the hospital. Why should we care for our emotional or mental wounds any differently than a physical one?

Forgiving yourself is like going to God's hospital with a deep infected wound. When someone wounds you and all you put on it is a band-aid, pretending like it never happened, an infection happens.

The infection is called unforgiveness, blame, revenge. It is a slow infectious process that might not have realized. The wound becomes festered, infiltrating the bloodstream. You finally go to the hospital, near death with sepsis. The doctor (God), must do the tedious and painful task of reopening the wound, draining it, and cleaning it out.

You stay and rest until you are doing well enough. The doctor sends you home with instructions on how to keep it clean, this time without a band-aid. He says, clean it with care, do not cover up and allow to heal from the inside out.

Soon the wound is completely healed and there are very little to no signs. This is when peace shows up. This peace is like nothing you have ever felt, it stretches beyond healing and self-care, and with it comes trust and honor.

When a wound happens at the hand of another, they are to blame but we are called to forgive and take care of ourselves through God. He is our peacemaker.

When peace comes, so does forgiveness toward others

> "Not seven times, but seventy times seven times!" Matthew 18:22

Forgiveness operates out of a repentant heart. All throughout the Word, it describes forgiveness alongside sin. God forgave our sins by sacrificing our Savior, and in that is our salvation. Salvation is having a repentant heart and turning away from sin to follow Jesus.

Forgiving others, as we have been forgiven.

For many of you, forgiveness has become a foul word, a mission that you must overcome. Forgiving a child molester, an abuser, a cheater, or a murderer, the list could go on. Maybe forgiveness has become a weighted blanket, something that you feel pressured into by other like a mantra over your life, heavy and burdensome.

It is very possible that the Church has unintentionally applied forgiveness to your life like it was a way to Heaven. Some Pastors may have told you that you aren't filled with enough grace after a divorce, or you aren't trying hard enough if someone had cheated on you.

Set aside all that you know or have been taught and allow the Word to be your guiding source of forgiveness. In Matthew 18, it describes Peter coming to Jesus and asking him how many times he should forgive an offender, "seven times?" Jesus answers him saying, "Not seven times, Peter, but seventy times seven times!" Jesus follows this with an example of a story on forgiveness.

When we don't forgive others who have hurt us, we sit complacent on the battle ground. Complacency in battle is death at the hand of the enemy. We must take a risk, and God has given us all we need in that risk.

Forgiveness is not acceptance

> *"Since we are now joined to Christ, we have been given the treasures of redemption by his blood-the total cancellation of our sins-all because of the cascading riches of his grace."* Ephesians 1:7-8

A person that has been abused, does not have to accept the abuse. Or, the adulterer's actions, an assault on their life, or a molestation. The purpose of forgiveness is not to accept the transgression but to bring restoration and healing. This is not only beneficial to your wellness but it hands over the sinner to God. In fact, those who refuse to forgive are not understanding how much of their own sin they need forgiven.

When Jesus tells us to forgive, it is not saying we accept the violations against us, but instead, we are releasing it all to God. You are saying, you will not hold on to the things that have been done to you, it is not yours to carry, and it is not your judgment to make. It has everything to do with your freedom.

Forgiving is not a quick phrase you say and hand it over to God, it is the calculated task of walking through every iniquity by the person that hurt you. Surrendering it all to the one who died for forgiveness.

Forgiveness is the cross in which Jesus died for us, forgiveness will never be acceptance, but it will always be sovereign.

Forgiving without return or reconciliation

> *"...Don't condemn others and you will not be condemned. Forgive over and over, and you will be forgiven over and over."* Luke 6:37

Jesus is and was and always will be the leading example of selfless love and forgiveness, His dying words he prayed over and over, "Father, forgive them for they don't know what they're doing."

Sometimes sitting with the person that brought you the deepest pain and going through the forgiveness process is not always going to turn out in the way we expect. But forgiving those who hurt you brings freedom and freedom is grace. Grace is God's heart, and His heart is relentless for you.

I remember having to go to court and stand up next to the person who had abused me. Even though he lived across the ocean and was only there for this court date, I was afraid for my life. The judge could see it and hear it, the control. When the court process was over, the court ordered the bailiff to walk the abuser out while I remained in the building.

Watching this man walk by me on his way out, I felt weak. This person tortured me for years, my soul held captive by his hands and his words. On my way out, I saw him sitting on the courthouse steps. Fear rising, my knees went weak and felt as though they would buckle beneath me.

Somehow finding the courage to speak to him, I said, "I forgive you."

Saying those words did not change the past, but it gave me freedom for the future and allowed God to show up through me without ever having had an apology from the other person.

Forgiveness is trusting the justice of God

> "And when you pray, make sure you forgive the faults of others
> so that your Father in heaven will also forgive you."
> Matthew 6:14

There are times when we must forgive those we may never see, but forgiving others is not about seeing the result. It is dying to yourself and believing that God has greater plans for your life than sitting in the need to know.

Forgiveness is trusting the outcome of what we cannot see, it is trusting in the justice of God. Trust requires consistency, growth, time, and a lot of work. Once you have forgiven, let go of all the things and put your trust into God.

You may not even understand all the reasons behind every offense, and we truly do not have the capacity to understand that which is not our own. Continue to be honest in all that you take to God, every way that you have been affected by the offender. Be aware of the deepest parts of the pain.

There was a time when I was getting my mail. It was like any other day, a completely monotonous routine. Flipping through the mail, was all the same, bills and junk. I noticed a handwritten letter addressed to me.

The name and the address on the letter triggered me. My hands trembled, the envelope falling out my fingers and on to the floor.

When I was married, my ex-husband had an affair. A long affair full of elaborate lies, telling her he was divorced, and we had a shared family home. She never doubted him and so when I was not home, she had full access to our home.

I imagined her riding in our family car, cooking in our kitchen, showering in our bathroom, and having sex in our marriage bed.

After the divorce, I received a call from the other woman, asking for the truth. I told her everything and despite the lies, she continued to stay with him. I do not know why this woman stayed, but in some respects, I related.

Opening the letter, I hoped for understanding, or an apology but most of all there was hope that she cared. There was nothing in the letter that was close to understanding, it was five full pages of judgement and condemnation. Line after line she verbally assaulted me, a full character assassination.

I sobbed on the bed as the weight of her words made their way toward my heart. Then, there was anger, with a vengeance, I roared loud! I slid down the bed onto the floor and sat in silence, as teared spilled out.

After pulling myself together, sitting back up on the bed, folding the letter back up. I could have called her or attacked back, there a lot of things I could have done in response to the anger raging inside.

Instead, I folded the letter neatly and put it back in the envelope. Got on my knees humbly before God. I prayed. Asking for forgiveness for thoughts I had toward her, and then I forgave her, before the face of Christ.

It was hard to accept the injustice that had been thrusted on my life, but the greatest vengeance was an act of love, forgiveness. I will never know what happened to her from the act of forgiveness but there have been many blessings bestowed on me by dying to myself and choosing forgiveness.

---

1. Start with sharing. Recognize the value of bringing offenses out and into the open. Be honest with God and yourself and then others, this shifts the victim mentality to accountability. Free yourself.

2. Are you on the pathway of unforgiveness? Continuing in bitterness, revenge and blaming it all on the offender? The only way off is to have one on one time with God. Spend an entire day off with the Lord, fasting and focused. Spend the day releasing yourself of unforgiveness and preparing for a journey through the healing process.

3. What are some of God's promises in forgiveness? Write a list of scripture and journal your responses to those promises. This entry will be a reminder to you as you prepare to walk through your forgiveness journey.

4. Are you ready to forgive? Although very challenging- Start by praying for the offender. Be the vessel of God's grace to those who have hurt you, bringing honor and glory to God and finding healing within yourself. All of this is not a means of acceptance, it is your freedom.

5. Let go and leave the justice up to God. Forgiving eliminates the internal dialogue that keeps you in charge of justice, speaking venom about another, or wanting revenge. Let it all go, give it to God so you can keep moving on the journey you were called to.

2

THE TRUTH: YOU ARE NOT WHAT HAPPENED TO YOU

"Beloved friends, if life gets extremely difficult, with many tests, don't be bewildered as though something strange were overwhelming you. Instead, continue to rejoice, for you, in a measure, have shared in the sufferings of the Anointed One so that you can share in the revelation of his glory and celebrate with even greater gladness!" 1Peter 4:12-13

WALKING IN TRUTH IS A BEAUTIFUL JOURNEY, BUT IT IS NOT WITHOUT ITS hardships, tests, and trials. God doesn't ever say, you will not go through things. He says, he will be there when you do. In fact, there are multiple accounts throughout the Bible that prove God shows up in tribulation.

Why Did This Happen?

> "…It happened to him so that you could watch him experience God's miracle" John 9:3

The question most often asked after a life of trauma is, "if God is so good, why did He allow this to happen to me? If God loved me, why did it happen? If you are God, where were you when I was in pain?" All these questions have one thing in common, the word "if."

"If" and "why" assume doubt. Doubt is a liar. The Bible tells us the truth. The truth is, God is good, He loves you, and God is near you. We find this truth through the Word of God, aligning ourselves with a new perspective and a new way of asking. Because this happened, what will God do through the suffering? When He heals me, how will He use me?

Because he is good, because he loves you, and because he is near you, he will use the trauma you went through to increase your dependence on Him through your faith in Him. It says in Romans chapter 5, "in times of trouble we have joyful confidence, knowing that our pressures will develop in us patient endurance. And patient endurance will refine our character, and proven character leads us back to hope. And this hope is not disappointing because we can now experience the endless love of God cascading into our hearts through the Holy Spirit."

Sometimes we have to let go of the need to know why it happened and trust that there is a greater plan that comes from the healing. God does not want us to suffer, He wants us to turn to him when bad things happen to us. He wants to move in the most miraculous and breathtaking ways, because he is good, and he loves us.

Once we stop asking why and start saying because, miraculous healing takes place, and we are used as a testimony of His goodness and grace.

I can attest to it all. God's goodness and love rescued me from the trauma I went through, and the lies that came with it. I do not ask God why it happened anymore. *The miraculous testimony of faith I walk in, is greater than the trauma I went through.*

What Are You Wearing?

> "Put on God's complete set of armor provided for us, so
> that you will be protected as you fight against the evil
> strategies of the accuser!" Ephesians 6:11

The very first chapter of the book, I shared a story of something traumatic happening to me but still had no memory of it. The lie that I continually told myself was, it never happened. The truth is something happened that day that did traumatize me. Without resources or counseling, I went into survival mode and created spaces and characters that clothed me in a false identity. When you put on the trauma like a fashion statement, instead of who you are designed to be, it is a faux identity.

Wearing the trauma that happened, is taking ownership of it. It can be recognized by the words you use. Do you find yourself saying things like, "my abuser" instead of the person who abused me? Or "my anxiety" instead of the anxiousness I struggle in? God told me, every time I took ownership of things that do not belong on me, I was wearing deception.

There came a point in my life when I allowed everyone else to tell me who I was and what happened to me. I didn't even remember what I looked like underneath it all. Which meant, every relationship I was in was based off this false identity.

Day by day, I put my trust in others, allowing them to dress me with this idea of who I was. As years went by, I was a pile of used, tattered, torn and dirty hand me down labels. But I believed to be wearing the very best because I believed more in what others put on me than who God said I was.

God has the best outfit for you! In fact, it is made for war.

The full armor of God in Ephesians chapter 6, the belt of truth, breastplate of righteousness, shoes of the gospel, shield of faith, helmet of salvation, and the sword of the spirit, is all we should be wearing. It is the only thing that protects us in battle. It does not say we will be without injury; it says our armor strengthens us to stand victorious.

Our battle was never against flesh and blood, it is against evil forces and when we wear the full armor of God, it keeps us standing alert and covers our heart.

Some of us will gain a brand-new armor, ready for battle. Others of us, may have to get our tarnished armor off the shelf, spending time polishing every crevice before we can put it on.

The armor of God deflects the enemy's arrows, you will no longer wear self-rejection, hatred, bitterness, insecurities, or suffering. Wear all things honorable, praiseworthy, forgiving, and holy. Time to take off what has happened to you and put on the full armor of God.

You are not defined by your past, confined by the present, or undetermined by the future

> "Though we experience every kind of pressure, we're not
> crushed. At times we don't know what to do, but quitting is
> not an option." 2 Corinthians 4:8

The whole book of Job gives us a greater understanding and depth of physical and spiritual suffering but remaining faithful in God. Job is a rich man, with a life that appears perfect, full of friends, riches, and family.

Job is tested by the enemy and becomes faced with much loss, suffering, and trauma. He loses everything and becomes physically ill but still refuses to blame God.

The whole book shows us that we can bring all our suffering to God, with steadfast hope, and completely trust that God knows exactly what He is doing. Even when Job cries out to God, and He doesn't answer, Job remains confident.

In the book of Job, chapter 23, Job says, "when I am tested, I will come out gold."

Gold can go through many things, even when stretched and beaten down to a thin sheet, it never loses its value.

Just like us, no matter the circumstances, when we are stretched, tested, and beaten, we will never lose our value. In the end, God restored all that Job lost and blessed him with twice as much.

We are not our past, we do not remain confined to our current circumstances either. God blesses the faithful with twice as much victory over the amount of trauma.

Understanding your inheritance

"Your faith in me has given you life. Now you may leave and walk in the ways of peace." Luke 7:50

We often undervalue ourselves by becoming what happened to us, but we are made righteous in Christ. You are set apart and made holy by salvation, not by what you do or has been done to you.

The story of Mary Magdalene in the Bible shows us what it looks like to come out of trauma and into a full inheritance. Mary was a deeply afflicted woman, who suffered from mental illness. But Jesus saw past it all, he saw her inheritance. A courageous and devoted woman, despite her afflictions. Mary had an inner gifting to minister; she would be a blessing to others.

In Luke chapter 7, Jesus was traveling and gaining popularity through his teaching and miracles. Miracles of freedom from suffering, the lame to walk, the blind to see, and leprosy. Many were coming to see Jesus, wanting to be by him, and some were inviting him into their home.

A Jewish leader, named Simon, was one who extended an invitation to Jesus. Simon was a pharisee, a very righteous leader that upheld the law. But Pharisee in the hidden places were self-indulgent and greedy leaders, who were religiously hypocritical of others, by priding themselves to be separate of sin while living in the hiddenness of sin.

It says, "Jesus took a place at the table." This moment was pivotal. Simon, an elite figure was inviting in Jesus of the people. The people had to be curious why Jesus would enter the house of the hated.

In the same neighborhood was Mary, when she heard Jesus was at Simon's house, she took the most expensive alabaster flask and filled it with a valuable perfume and walked to the home of Simon.

Mary walked into the room uninvited, breaking barriers, and knelt at the foot of Jesus. Crying, she took down her hair, wiped away her tears, kissed the feet of Jesus. Then, she breaks open the bottle ad anoints him with a year's worth of wages in perfume.

When Simon saw this happen, he was thinking to himself if Jesus was a true prophet, he would never allow a sinner to touch his feet. Jesus responded to the thoughts of Simon, describing the neglect that he received as a guest of the home and table. But this woman had the courage to show up in a home, uninvited, and greet him respect.

Mary was forgiven of her sins that day. She knew her inheritance, bringing the best and the worst of herself to the table. Through an extravagant display of love, she gathered all that she had, including the shame and labels thrust on her by others, and walked into a room of judgement to lay it at the foot of Jesus.

She was not a victim; the power of the Holy Spirit overcame her, and she became a woman who knew she was worthy of her true identity. She was not what happened to her, but she was a woman delivered of demons and a woman who came into her full inheritance, a ministering woman of God. Not defined by her afflictions but defined by grace, Mary went on to follow Jesus all the way to his death and resurrection.

The only way for her to anoint Jesus with the perfume, was to break the neck of the alabaster bottle. Both the perfume and the bottle were expensive, a year's worth of wages. But the bottle was most valuable when it was broken, it was in the brokenness that the fragrance of her full inheritance was released.

Come into your full inheritance, with unwavering loyalty and faith, walk through the room and take your rightful place at the table. Bring everything that you have, the best and the worst, break it all open and pour it at his feet. Get up from there and walk with Jesus into who you are.

Who you are, the truth

> "You've set me free, and now I'm standing complete..." Psalm
> 18:36

You are limitless, inherently through Christ. Jesus sets a path that compels us to walk in our identity. Years ago, God prepared a way for me through an identity conversation. Who we are does not call for acceptance of the world, but instead humbles us to embrace ourselves in our own unique identity. In the embrace, we come to understand the vision God has for us.

He had me draw out four circles. Three smaller circles around a large circle. One circle, God had me list all the things that would describe my character, hobbies and likes. From songs to clothing, movies, and places of travel. Another circle, He had me list relationally. Connections, friendships, social settings, etc. The last circle, He had me write all the traumatic events. Assaults, offenses, abuse, etc.

In the largest circle, I wrote the word, "Christ." Under the word Christ, I wrote the words WHOLE, HEALED, and WITH PURPOSE.

God pointed out the three circles and told me, the list within those circles were built of desires, preferences, and pain. The three circles would change with age, experience, circumstances, social setting, and healing. The circles were not my identity but had become it with every passing season. Basing your identity in something that is ever changing or wrapped up in what has been done to us through trauma, violence, assault, or pain, has the potential to cause a lot of additional and unnecessary pain.

Then, God pointed to the larger circle and said, "be liberated by wearing only one identity, Christ, the unique expression of God."

When God led me through the book of Zechariah in the Bible, a nine-chapter story of freedom from suffering, I read the story of people who were taken into captivity. Suffering every day but giving into their suffering and becoming the environment in which, they lived.

These people gave up hope on breaking free from their captivity and their own identity was the captivity in which they lived, even though God promised their freedom. When God did come and free them, some people did not want to leave.

Choosing to stay in suffering because the trauma has become your identity, means you are choosing captivity over the greater freedom He promised you.

You are whole and healed

"His love broke open the way, and he brought me into a beautiful, broad place. He rescued me-because his delight is in me!" Psalm 18:19

There should never be a day when you wake up and say, "I am done working on myself." We always have work to do within, God is continuously growing you and going after that growth no matter what. There will be a day you wake up and say, I am healed!

When we have traumatic and painful things happen in our life, whether they are small or large, it has the potential to hinder our identity in Christ. It is a vital part of the healing process to turn it over to God because the enemy wants us to be in our pain, he wants us focused on the symptoms and diagnosis.

The hinderance is not the symptoms from trauma, it is how we respond in them. When we put all our focus on the physical aspect of the pain we endured because of trauma, we are lifting the offender into a place of worship and the offense becomes an idol in our lives.

This becomes a spiritual symptom; the enemy wants to keep us out of the healing process. Because the process leads us to a life of purpose in Jesus, but you are made whole and promised healing through him.

Stay in the presence of the spiritual. In Ephesians 6 it says, "Your hand-to-hand combat is not with human beings, but with the highest principalities and authorities operating in rebellion under the heavenly realms. For they are a powerful class of demon-gods and evil spirits that hold this dark world in bondage."

There are many of us who will continue to struggle through a diagnosis and continue to need proper resources or treatment to carry us through. However, you can be healed and still be in a recovery journey. It has been my experience through the years, many who shift their focus to becoming spiritually healed in Christ, will see their physical healing take place and the symptoms of trauma dissipate (some immediately and others a process).

Believe you are healed! One of the most critical stumbling blocks in our healing process is doubt and doubt is a liar. Invite Jesus into your moments of doubt through prayer. Remain in the voice of God and not the voice of others, he will always impart the truth.

I am a Christian woman that struggles with anxiety, which seems to allow room for people to refute: "Hah! God isn't real." "Why aren't you healed then?" "Pray differently," or "pray more."

Anxiety is not a direct reflection of my faith, but my response to it is. Anxiety doesn't make me any less faithful, it is a journey of self-discovery and intentionally built moments with God. It is important to know that while we are afflicted, God meets us there.

I am a healed woman by the stripes and blood of Jesus, declaring me righteous. To be righteous is the promise of peace and authority over afflictions. My gratitude for this truth ignites a hope, hope reminds me that I can move in confidence of God's love that surpasses the symptom of anxiety.

I am made whole in Christ; He is the owner and creator of all things, including language and defining language. He turns anxiety into anticipation and triggers into activation.

Continue to work on yourself by the means in which are healthy for your growth, whether its seeking counsel or having a treatment plan, diet, exercise, or art therapy. Walk confidently in your spiritual healing and believe in who you are, respond to symptoms that arise with the power of prayer and praise. Eliminate doubt and surround yourself with core people who will keep encouraging you to stand in the Word of God.

You are with purpose

> "So don't hide your light! Let it shine brightly before others, so
> that your commendable works will shine as a light upon
> them, and then they will give their praise to your Father in
> heaven." Matthew 5:16

You can be actively going through or out of trauma and still walk with purpose. This may seem way out of reach when you are feeling exhausted and weak, but it states in the Bible that you find power in your weakness through the strength of God, His strength is sufficient to carry you through anything.

Jesus taught us how to live a life of purpose through all things, in Matthew 5.

Jesus is sitting on the mountainside, overlooking a crowd of people. He begins to teach the people their purpose, a sort of discipleship training course. He doesn't start by asking if you want a purpose and he doesn't ask what your purpose will be. He shares what will become of you IN your purpose.

He tells us who we will be, what will happen when we walk in it, and the reward at the end of it all.

• WE WILL BE:

Happy
Delighted
Blessed
Enriched
Satisfied
Joyful

• WHEN WE:

Turn to Him
Wait on Him
Live in gentleness
Crave righteousness
Are merciful
Are pure and peaceful
Bear the weight of persecution and insult

Our reward is greater than the cost of walking with purpose. We will reap the harvest of the things that hurt us when we walk with purpose. The very first thing he rewards us with, is the Heaven Kingdom and in this, we find all that we long for.

• Rewards of:

Mercy
Fruitfulness
Recognition
More of God

Jesus leaves us with a choice. He isn't demanding us to take a position of purpose, but if we choose to walk with purpose, our lives will be enriched through it.

I have had to continue and walk in purpose despite any residual or current trauma that came up. Jesus said in the sermon on the mount, we will gain persecution, cruel lies, insults all why loving Him. I choose to grow every day in and through it all. Not allowing my identity to be wrapped up in what happened to me or what will happen to me.

The enemy makes it so easy to hate, but the Bible tells us to let love, above all else, be the beautiful reward for which we move in. It is from the depths of Christ's love, in which we are motivated by all things.

1. Grab a sheet of paper or your journal. Split the paper into four sections with a line down the middle. On the left side, write a list of all the times you cried out "if only" or "why?" when something painful has happened to you. On the left middle, next to that list all, write the doubt and fears it has created. On the right middle, change the narrative to "because He___." And, on the far-right side, write a scripture to back up your "because."

2. What have you taken ownership of that does not belong on you? Spend some time putting on the full armor of God.

3. What has defined you from your past or confined you in the present moment?

4. What does it mean for you to come into your full inheritance? What would it cost you to bring all you have to the foot of Jesus? When you have done this, write a journal of your process so you have something to reflect on.

5. Draw out three small circles, label the first one character, hobbies, and likes. The second one labeled relationally, friendships, community, and social setting. The third one labeled traumatic or painful events. Write a list in each one identifying these things about you. Then put a larger circle on the page and label it Christ. List who you are in Christ without any of the other labels. The hope is that the list in the larger circle would be more defined than the three smaller ones. If it is not, the journey begins today.

3

THE TRUTH: IT IS OK TO NOT BE OK

"Love empowers us to fulfill the law of the Anointed One as we carry each other's troubles" Galatians 6:2

Throw off the safety blanket

"People lose their way without wise leadership, but a nation succeeds and stands in victory when it has many good counselors to guide it." Proverbs 11:14

Every one of my kids had a stuffed animal that symbolized their safety blanket. One of my daughters carried hers with her everywhere, she named it "Nammy." Nammy was her comfort and security, it was the essence of her.

Nammy went on every vacation with us, including restaurants and movies, but was most effective at the end of every night when she needed to sleep. It had become her comfort for uncertain times or brand-new situations and places.

There came a time when her little Nammy became worn down to the stuffing, missing its buttons and barely able to sustain itself any longer.

My daughter finally had to lay her stuffed animal inside a protective box. A place where she cannot see it, but it is within distance to pull out and look at every now and then. A reminder of her growth but also how well she is moving on without it.

Once my daughter put her Nammy in a box, she was forced to turned toward her parents. Seeking out her father in times of tears or fear. Sitting in the room with me and her siblings and learning to communicate through her uncertain times.

These moments strengthened and empowered her to know, when she is in pain or uncertainty, she had her family.

Safety blankets have been around for years, giving children a sense of attachment, security, and comfort. They are used to cover and create a safer environment, in fact, they have been around for so long, nobody questions their use. We simply look at a child with their blanket and move on, never asking why they have one.

The use of the words "I am fine" has become just like a safety blanket. Or, like my daughter's Nammy, it becomes the essence of who we are, and we take it with us everywhere for every situation.

I read a survey online at the Mental Health Foundation, it said, "the average adult says they are fine as an automatic response several times throughout the week." The survey also revealed that most people were lying about it.

It is really fascinating that more than half of the adults asking how someone is doing, has an expectancy to hear someone is fine and will settle with that response.

There are a few reasons why "I am fine" or "It is fine" has become the automatic response of our lives;

- We say it to avoid an honest answer
- We do not want to be a burden with the truth
- Our truth has the potential to cause conflict
- It is a coping mechanism
- We simply do not want to answer or have the time to answer

There comes a time in our lives where our safety blanket will become so worn out it is hanging by a thread. A time when we must store it away in a safe place. Not too far but close enough to remind us of the truth, we never needed it for all the things we thought we did.

Turning to our father and then community, when we are in pain and uncertainty, will strengthen and empower us to move on. The essence of who you are is not in the security of "I am fine." It is not in anything outside of God.

Needing help is not a burden

> "Your plans will fall apart right in front of you if you fail to get good advice..." Proverbs 15:22

Sometimes we think the burden of the truth is too large for people to handle, we begin to avoid or sabotage friendships. Assuming others response to our truth, creates an extremely passive and effortless way to handle what we are going through. Ultimately, we will end up isolating ourselves.

There is a huge difference between getting alone with God and isolating ourselves with the purpose of avoiding or hiding from the truth. Avoiding people because of the possibility of something, is not healthy.

It starts with you. The probability of finding strength and healing in bringing the truth to light is far greater than losing everything over it. Do not wait until the aftermath to tell them you went through something.

If you are going through trauma and someone asks you how you are doing, tell the short truth: "I am not well." Assess their response and then ask them a question back, "can I open up to you?" This gives them the chance to make their own decision on whether they want to engage in an honest conversation.

And, on the flip side. Be aware of asking others how they are doing and prepare to answer with an open heart, ready for conversation. It is in the undoing of these poor and burdensome habits that we will learn empathy and understanding. Slowing down for a moment and genuinely engaging the question we are asked or are asking of someone, "How are you?"

I am not OK, and here is why...

> *"Love empowers us to fulfill the law of the Anointed One as we*
> *carry each other's troubles." Galatians 6:2*

I am fine is sometimes used as a coping mechanism to avoid conflict, especially when the person asking if we are okay is the person that hurt you.

This is one of the greatest opportunities to become both the healer and the one who will be healed. Stepping into a place of empathy after someone hurt you, so long as the person that the conflict is with is not a deep affliction that needs therapy but is something that can be nurtured back to health through community and healthy conversation.

Empathy is not coming into agreement with the conflict, it is setting all conclusions aside about the person that hurt you by understanding that they may be coming from a pained place as well. View them through the heart of God.

Move into a position of love, for yourself and the other person.

There is always the potential for judgement when we open ourselves up for healing with other people, but we must assume that others have our best interest because it gives God the opportunity to move in and through the conflict and you learn to appreciate the person on the other end.

Redefining the way we answer how we are, especially in the middle of conflict, can trigger an anxious response. Leading us back to auto response, I am fine.

I remember the first time I stepped out of auto response and answered with the truth. I was in a house full of people I was still growing to trust, a few of them were people who had unintentionally hurt me. It was a moment of great tension, but I still found myself answering "I am not okay, and here is why..."

God opened the door in that moment. The room shifted, everyone leaned in and created space for me to open up. I spent the next two hours sharing my heart. It was messy and all over the place, but they stayed with me in it all.

To this day, when they ask me how I am doing. I answer honestly.

Not every honest answer is a conflict resolution, or a sit down and hash it out. But every honest answer is met with validation. This creates a trusted space, always keeping lines of communication open, where both the person asking and the person answering gain a healthy and safe relationship.

An honest answer on the go

"Speaking honestly is a sign of true friendship." Proverbs 24:26

It is okay to say you are fine when this is a genuine response and not an excuse to move on. If you are fine, then you are fine!

A lot of times we have strangers on the street, or people coming into our workplace that we do not even know, asking us how we are doing for the day. We must keep accountability flowing both ways and shift the momentum of answering, I am fine, as a habit.

It goes both ways, slow down and give a moment to the person asking and give yourself the opportunity to be honest. There are many ways to answer honestly and keep it short without throwing the stranger off guard.

A great example of answering honestly but eliminating responsibility of the person asking is, "It's a rough day but I am pulling through." Keeping it surface level, without details and ending your response with the work you are putting into it keeps it lighthearted, honest and without work on the receiving end.

Change the course

"Your great faithfulness is infinite, stretching over the whole earth." Psalm 36:5

Be a person that changes the course and start asking how someone is, with the intent of receiving more than "I am fine" as an answer.

When asking someone if they are okay, keep it light and gentle, do not press them but allow space for them to answer with honesty. Often, I hear they are fine, and I respond with, "That's great. But if you ever have a bad day, I'm here to listen."

It takes consistency to break habit.

There was a time my daughter was playing at the beach and a bunch of little butterflies were gathering around her.

Completely unaware, she kept digging in the sand as we all gathered around to see the phenomenon. Suddenly, a little butterfly landed on her shoulder, and she looked at it with surprise. She smiled, then just as quickly, she started to panic.

She yelled, "Get off, get off. No!" I asked her if she wanted help.

She didn't answer, then she started to self-soothe. "It's okay. It is going to be okay. It is just a flutterby."

She calmed down some, but I saw she was still very uncomfortable. I asked again, are you okay? This time, she asked if I would remove the butterfly from her shoulder.

When we give the opportunity for the person to answer and they turn us away, but we still see them in obvious distress, assess the situation giving them opportunity to answer or work it out and then come back again with a gentle nudge. It is often, the second time you ask, they let you in.

----

1. Are you leaning on "I am fine" as a security blanket? Which bullet points do you fall under?

2. Can you think of times where you have held back an honest answer because you felt like a burden? Write down some of those times and assess what shut you down. How could you have responded differently?

3. Can you think of current or past situations where conflicts have arisen and you did not answer honestly? How will you respond differently in the future?

4. Write examples of how you can respond honestly to someone you do not know.

THE TRUTH: YOU ARE WORTHY AND YOU ARE SEEN

"With this in mind, we constantly pray that our God will empower you to live worthy of all that he has invited you to experience. And we pray that by his power all the pleasures of goodness and all works inspired by faith would fill you completely." 2 Thessalonians 1:11

I ABSOLUTELY LOVE THAT GOD HAS CHALLENGED MY TRUTH BY EMPOWERING me to live worthy, with an invitation to experience Him and all He has for us. Of all the definable words that have been thrown at us, the word "worthy" seems to be the most conflicting of them all. Many people I have worked with have stated they feel unworthy but when asked how they define this word, they get stuck.

It is a great life challenge to move forward in worthiness if we do not understand what that means. An even greater challenge when the Bible mentions worthy almost a hundred times in scripture and you aren't living out your day to day walk in a way that corresponds to the calling on your life.

Worth versus Worthy

"But Christ proved God's passionate love for us by dying in our place while we were still lost and ungodly!" Romans 5:8

First, let's distinguish the difference between worth and worthy, in the context of the Bible. The origin of the word, "worth", in the Bible means, value. Our value, per God, is priceless. First, we are inherently given worth from the time of our creation and then our redemption at the cross was the final cost to have everlasting life, a value that cannot be undone.

The Hebrew word for worthy means, seen or possessing a merit of excellence. And walking in worthiness means to hold a high level of respect and dignity, all in the name of glorifying God.

It is natural when we are younger and impressionable, to turn to others for our worth. Children often learn their value at school and among peers. Social media today is one of the top-rated voices of self-worth.

If you did not have a healthy family or school life, without intentional and deliberate empowerment of true sense of self-worth, you have a whole journey of undoing the lies. But the good news is that it can all be done through the understanding that our worth (being seen as worthy) has absolutely nothing to do with others and everything to do with God.

Our value, how we are seen, and the worthiness in which we are called to walk in, comes in the form of dignity. Redeemed by Christ and in union with God, having been made in His likeness, we are a kingdom family and called to walk at this level of honor.

If we live from the world view, from violations or humiliation against us, there is the potential to feel as though we have lost our self-worth and dignity. However, because of the cross, we cannot lose or be stripped of it.

Living worthy is nourishment to our potential

> *"For through the eternal and living Word of God you have been born again. And this "seed" that he planted within you can never be destroyed but will live and grow inside of you forever." 1 Peter 1:23*

Though completely undeserving, we will always be worthy. Worthiness is like a dormant seed that is waiting to be nourished to life, it can stay that way for years until cultivated and brought to the surface where it receives sun (Jesus) and water (Baptism).

Jesus releases every possibility when you entrust in him, he is the nutrients to our growth when we build an everlasting relationship with time and care. Reading the word, in prayer, and worship, or spending alone time with him, activates us in a way that keeps us driven to stay alive through nourishment.

When the conditions change around us, threatening our growth and potential harvest, refuse to be intimidated by the odds. Challenge yourself to remain worthy.

Live worthy by pouring into all that God has given you. Rather than struggling to keep yourself alive, you will reap a harvest that feeds a multitude, and this is your greatest potential.

A life of potential that doesn't merely exist but is excited to live in what is next. It is moving in things you have yet to accomplish, through God's will. If we do not live according to His will, we are limiting access to the signs, wonders, and miracles of God.

We are all gifted, limitless in His power and strength, no longer dormant but alive and able to produce a harvest of potential in living a life worthy to the call.

You are seen by your empowerment team

> *"But God has carefully designed each member and placed it in the body to function as he desires." 1 Corinthians 12:18*

Build on your empowerment team! To have an amazing team with core people, build on what God is giving you and not what you want. If you are lacking a team of people who are loyal, trustworthy, and can encourage you, you may have to see what is keeping you from engaging. Look at what is influencing you toward the "wrong" team and what is keeping you away from the "right" team.

- Comparison is a killer
- Rejection projection
- Trusting the wrong team

One of the greatest conflicts that goes on between others is, comparison. Comparison is first a thief, stealing joy and value and then when it is done with you, it kills your spirit. The root of comparison is jealousy.

All these things point to a sign that says, "God does not have enough for me" but when we walk in worthiness, we know that God brings us favor. First, find the point of discontentedness and dissatisfaction in your own life and turn it over to gratitude.

Gratitude activates the brain by boosting serotonin and producing dopamine, which creates joy. One of the many benefits of joy is building and maintaining healthy relationships through care and reciprocation.

Another thing that can get in the way of your empowerment team is **rejection projection**, and this comes from trauma we received from consistent rejection in our lives. We have begun to build off of coping mechanisms instead of a team of people that will empower us.

This can be recognized through automatic negative thoughts such as, others don't want you or like you. You will avoid them or go completely opposite and please them instead of working on a healthy team relationship. This all stems from misunderstanding your worth. The projection of this type of trauma is to take the parts of yourself that you feel are unworthy and place it on the other person through denial, anger, or avoidance.

The alternate form of lacking a power team, is trusting in the wrong one. You have such low self-worth you pick anyone who will say yes. This inevitably ends up hurting everyone involved. The telling signs of an unhealthy team is being agreeable to everyone else, which can lead you into places that go against everything you were designed to do and then you feel responsible for it all. Other signs are not speaking up about hurts, pains, or conflict just to keep the peace.

Once you have built off an unhealthy team, it is very difficult to break free, but it is possible with God.

Trusting the wrong team is like playing in the wrong sandbox. Picture two sandboxes, one is full of toys that seem fun and desirable to your eye and the other one has no toys but a table, it appears to be less desirable. God says, hey I have a sandbox for you and points to the one with the table, but it is already too late you are running toward the one with the toys in it.

Problem is, the one with the toys is a mirage, it is quicksand and once you jump in, every move you make will tighten and squeeze around you until you cannot breathe. The only way out, is to hold still and allow God to pull you out.

An unhealthy team is very much like the box with toys in it, it looks like fun, but it is quicksand and will tighten and squeeze you until you can't breathe. The other box is the one God is calling you to, had you gone and sat in it, you would find yourself soon surrounded by others brought in by God.

An empowering team will bring you self-awareness, communicate with you and see you as God does. If you do not have those people, it is time to set boundaries and work toward the ones that God has called to you.

Boundary to build on

> "So above all, guard the affections of your heart, for they affect
> all that you are. Pay attention to the welfare of you
> innermost being, for from there flows the wellspring of life."
> Proverbs 4:23

Many of us cringe to think about boundary setting, especially when it someone very close to us. But, if we shift our perspective toward Jesus, a leading example in boundaries setting to build on to live out a kingdom mindset. A kingdom mindset is a person that has their priorities on seeking first God and living with truth, humility, purpose, and obedience.

With our minds set on these things, we can set boundaries with anyone for any reason.

Jesus took a lot of time away to be alone with God. I was once reading over a timeline of the journey of Jesus, when God showed me that Jesus spent more time in rest and on the road with his empowerment team than he spent in ministry. When he took the time, he didn't ask, he simply went. This kept him and his response, kind and compassionate.

Jesus also showed us that saying no is okay too. He didn't always say yes to every request and often when he did say yes, he would guide them to be a part of their own growth.

Boundaries are for meeting your personal needs, getting alone with God to nourish those needs, and receiving healthy support. And, for the other person, it is offering grace for choices (with consequences) that bring health to your relationship. Regardless of their response to your boundary, we continue to love. Not enforce or control.

The best places to build on boundary setting are situations that have been demanding, abusive, or manipulative. It is important to be accountable to each situation, take only what belongs to you through your thoughts, choices, and feelings.

You can remain neutral in boundary building asking yourself a few questions, what does the other person really want from me, what outcome do I want from this, and am I worth it?

You are worthy, you are seen, and you are loved! Regardless of what the world wants you to think, your life matters!

---

1. Write out several points of scripture where God describes worthiness.

2. Is your worthiness dormant? What areas of life do you need to bring to the surface and nourish for a greater walk of worthy?

3. Are you surrounded by a healthy team? Write down the core people in your life that lift you up, value your input, create space for improvement, communicate well in conflict and hold you accountable.

4. Are there areas where you need to break free from unhealthy relationships and build on your team? Expand on your boundary setting.

5

THE TRUTH: YOU ARE QUALIFIED
EVERYTHING YOU DO MATTERS TO HIM AND YOU NEED A SUPPORT SYSTEM

"Yet we don't see ourselves as capable enough to do anything in our own strength, for our true competence flows from God's empowering presence." 2 Corinthians 3:5

Heart first before circumstances

"So everyone should continue to live faithful in the situation of life in which they were called to follow Jesus" 1 Corinthians 7:20

One of the biggest lies about salvation is that you must suddenly become this well behaved, "perfect" Christian. Jesus called you out right where you were. He wants to transform you, not change you, for it is through your transformation that you are changed.

Don't let a lifestyle keep you from saying yes to a love of a lifetime.

In fact, many times people will hesitate to surrender their life to Jesus because they think they must give up everything all at once. The truth is, when you invite Jesus into your life, your life shifts in accordance with the journey he takes you on. In the shifting, things change as you go. Transforming your life through obedience and conviction, with intention and unintentionally, you will one day look back and see how your life has changed without even knowing!

There were so many times I ignored God because I wasn't ready to give up friends I hung out with, places I went to, clothes I wore, or the alcohol I drank. When I tried quitting it all for appearances and good works, I was overwhelmed and found myself falling back into old patterns. However, the moment I showed up broken, transformation began, and I was able to move with peace through old patterns and into new ones.

Our brokenness is when His power is made strong, and our transformation is certain in our weakness because it is the heart of kingdom living. He wants our heart, first transforming us from the inside to become like Jesus. It isn't about "acting right," it is about the fruit.

A heart transformation is a repentant one. First, knowing the difference between guilt and shame. Guilt is one of conviction; it is not dwelling but being accountable for your sins and takes a lot of honesty and humility before God. Shame is something the enemy wants to keep you in, trying to separate you from Jesus.

Next, do not focus on your failures more than your growth. Trust God in the process by continuing to build a relationship with Him, it is in the relationship that you will come to understand why you have sinned, and He will guide you and teach you to grow through every part of your life.

Last, understand repentance. Walk through Scripture and learn what God says about the importance of your heart transformation journey— bringing everything to the surface and into the light. Once your heart is set in motion, your circumstances will begin changing all around you.

Not every fight is yours; fight the right fight

> *"So now the case is closed. There remains no accusing voice of condemnation against those who are joined in life-union with Jesus, the Anointed One." Romans 8:1*

We do not have to fight our way to qualification, we are qualified through salvation. Jesus liberates us from law of sin because it limited us by our own weakness. We are free to live in full acceptance of the Spirit, and the Holy Spirit motivates us to pursue all things of God through Christ.

Resistance to the Spirit is your biggest warfare, it is when we die to ourselves that we gain authority. In Romans 8 it says we did not receive a spirit of religious duty. Mature children of God are those that are moved by the Holy Spirit, qualifying us to share our inheritance.

I have been moved by the Spirit since a very young age, I just did not know what it was. Every move I made was so unique and outside the traditional law of religion that I grew up in that I was often silenced or shut out. This caused so much rejection, I turned against everything. Fighting and bucking up against religious duty as if it was the Holy Spirit and leaving Church behind claiming, everything they did was God himself.

But my fight was not against religion or Church, it was the spiritual bondage that was keeping me in resistance to the Holy Spirit and fulfilling my purpose. The fight to hide and keep silent was more detrimental to me than the rejection and wounding I felt in the Church. I ended up in a community of spiritual seekers instead of spiritual movers. The enemy called me in, wrapped me up and promised me lies in the name of truth.

But God says nothing (or no *one*) has power over us.

My attachment to the idea that Church was God himself, created a lie that meant I would never measure up to who God says I was. This was a distraction from my true qualification as a frontline warrior. God had purposely placed my gifted life right in the middle of a Baptist community, an emotional young lady that had dreams, vision, and a voice for things about to happen.

The Church was not my qualifier, and their legalistic points of view were not holding me back. Not every space, community, or Church is an evil force out to get you. God placed me right where I needed to be: a purposeful, planned-out foundation and training ground for something greater in my life.

Without the foundation of Church and some of the rejections I went through, I would not have had my eyes opened to fight for who God made me to be.

He qualifies the called, Everything you do matters to Him

*"Having determined our destiny ahead of time, he called us to
himself and transferred his perfect righteousness to everyone
he called. And those who possess his perfect righteousness he
co-glorified with his Son!" Romans 8:30*

Jesus gives us a powerful example of standing firm in our qualification even while being rejected and shut down. In Luke 20, Jesus was preaching. A few high priests—the experts in religious law—confronted Jesus, asking him what authority he had to preach in the temple. Jesus responded by asking them if John baptized because of mandate of heaven or men. The high priests pulled back and discussed in private. Afraid to answer, they came up with nothing. Jesus declined to answer them as well.

It appears the high priests were more interested in the credentials of Jesus than the important message he was called to give. As a result, they tried to trap him with questions of authority.

Jesus was preaching without a degree or permission, and this was considered rebellious to the priests. Jesus put a stop to these religious experts by showing they were standing in legalism. What a considerable loss for these priests. While they were focused on the religious law, they missed the true message from God.

Christ stepped out that day so you could step in, setting a path of authority to preach God's message. A message that is breath and life, no age limit, no gender or race, a gospel that has no degree or certification. God's message is sanctification, and that is for everyone.

Step out of disqualification by shifting from who you are not, into who you are. Jesus did not call unto the qualified, he qualifies you who are already called.

For years I was convinced I had to prove myself to Church leadership. I was raised in an environment where there was no allowance for my position as a woman who wanted to preach or speak to God's people. When I finally came back to Church, I hid behind who I wasn't and surrendered to the will of Church leadership instead of God's will.

I spent years trying to qualify myself into places I did not belong, trying to prove myself in ministry and leadership with every move. This caused more rejection and tearful nights crying in my husband's arms. I was blaming leadership, living in offense and often distrust, but God stayed with me through it all because everything we do matters to Him. But imagine what can be done when we do what matters to Him!

In Romans 8:28 it says, *"...every detail of our lives is continually woven together for good, for we are his lovers who have been called to fulfill his designed purpose."*

Even in choosing to be in places for the wrong reason, God was able to use me according to His purpose. It wasn't until I was painfully shaken by the words of a close Church leader, that I realized what I was doing. I was more afraid of losing a position I never had, than I was concerned with losing their friendship. I set out to turn my face toward God and live a life fulfilling His design.

I remember a moment when I brought my fears of becoming a woman preacher/prophet to my brother, someone whose wisdom I respect very much. He asked me why I thought I couldn't do it. My answer was rejection based. He simply stated, "What God calls you into, no man can stop." That simple statement was the catalyst that kept me moving in the call on my life.

I knew a shift toward obedience would be hard. It always is when you build your life around your will and not God's. Taking yourself out of a place that many people have grown accustomed to is very difficult, especially when you have built your life surrendering to the call of another's life. Family, friends, and community may not be prepared for such a great shift, but there is an even greater reward in restoring who you are in Him.

God has reawakened the leader in me, the leader that cannot stand silent in injustices. I am called to speak, teach, and awaken the masses to the voice of God. I am a leader who will speak out encouragement, discerning what belongs to God and what does not. The leader who helps the broken and oppressed, leading them through transformation with teaching of scripture, intercession, and vision. I honor the gift of dreams and wisdom. I will always step out by the command of His voice even when it is awkward, uncomfortable, or misunderstood.

Your faith is the lead to the call on your life, your qualification is as strong as your faith. Who does God say you are?

Independence does not mean without leadership

> *"Don't forget the example of your spiritual leaders who have spoken God's messages to you, take a close look at how their lives ended, and then follow their walk of faith" Hebrews 13:7*

Sometimes, when we have gained so much momentum in the independent call on our life, we can often find our lives swinging hard and fast toward loneliness, sin, corruption. It is an important part of discipleship to commit to accountability within leadership.

Often, if you are called to ministry and leadership and you have just come out of a hostile environment, it creates a futile independence. A rogue leader is one who is afraid of being controlled. However, if you are called into ministry and leadership, it is especially important to check in for feedback and effectiveness.

It is important to not just have an empowerment team, but also a team of leadership that can come into alignment with the call on your life. A leadership that doesn't control you, but can align with your goal, respect your obedient posture, and still be able to stand in honesty and faith when you are being deceived.

The more honest you are, the stronger the faith your accountability team will have in you. There is safety in honesty because it exposes all agendas, removes every reason for personal attack or lies to fill the unknown spaces.

I spent many years running from Church, coming back to Church, surrendering who I was to leadership through the guise of volunteering and servanthood. Being under the care of leadership in my home Church was good, but I had become root bound and unable to grow into the role God wanted me in. I was convinced my leadership did not have my best interest by keeping me in in the small little planter box called "volunteer."

Then I was reawakened as a leader. I was concerned the safety of my newfound independence would be stripped of me, and so I went rogue out of fear. I was afraid of control, that they would put me back into the little planter box. The unknown spaces created lies. Those lies turned to offenses, competition, and a serious lack of faith for the journey God had me on.

It all changed when I went to my husband with concern and protection for the awakening of leadership in me. Together, we met with trusted leadership, and spoke honestly about some of our struggles. I decided to take eight weeks off Church, mentoring, ministry, and community to listen to God only.

It was during those eight weeks and the protection of my husband, the honesty with leadership and my empowerment team, that my life began changing in unexpected ways. God met me at every turn.

I had four specific God encounters because of leaning into his voice, learning who I was in Him, and being up front and surrounding myself in the safety of leadership that would align with what He was saying to me. All four encounters were with men, and all four encounters were with the purpose of restoring and building my trust within Church leadership.

God reminded me with every encounter that I had authority, and I was a mighty woman of God who was called and qualified for such a time as this. In eight weeks, I was surrounded by my best friend, Ashley, and my husband, Cody, two leadership team members, and my core empowerment team.

Independence in your call gains greater strength when surrounded by people who align with what God is saying to you. Aligning isn't always agreeing, it is simply keeping you accounted for in the kingdom of God. For me, it was taking me out of the planter box and putting me into kingdom soil. I remained planted at home, but my roots were free to stretch far and wide.

---

1. Are you allowing things in your life to hold you back? Write a list of personal convictions in your life that are keeping you from a total heart transformation. Take a repentance journey with God through Scripture. Allow Him to transform your heart by bringing things out into the open and walking with Jesus through it all.

2. Are there areas in your life you have been resisting the Spirit? What battles are you facing? Write them down and find scriptures that are weapons for the battle. Did you find any battles that are not your own?

3. Who does God say you are? Are there places in your life that need to shift out of who you are *not* and back into who you *are*? What gifts have you been given that are designed for His purpose?

4. Do you have leadership you can lean on? Find a safe place of accountability. It's not always someone who agrees with you, but one that can align with you and your growth in the call on your life.

6

THE TRUTH: YOU ARE NOT TOO MUCH
AND YOU ARE ENOUGH

"You are to love the Lord Yahweh, your God, with a passionate heart, from the depths of your soul, with your every thought, and with all your strength. This is the great and supreme commandment." Mark 12:30

The burden bearer, the passionate pursuer and the internal processor

"God always makes his grace visible in Christ, who includes us as partners of his endless triumph. Through our yielded lives he spreads the fragrance of the knowledge of God everywhere we go." 2 Corinthians 2:14

We are all made in the image of God, and that includes every emotion. However, outside of God, our emotions can turn to feelings that run away from us. We must take our feelings and cast them into the care of the Spirit, where they are cautiously tended to.

Emotions are necessary to fully experience life. They draw us closer to God than just our belief in Him. But even though we need our emotions, we cannot allow them to control or dictate what we do, and we cannot put all our trust into them.

Inviting the Spirit into our emotions means we gain authority over them. And when we're in the midst of *feeling*, our truth can be determined through the Spirit.

The lies that come in unhealthy or mislead emotions are:

- Too much
- Too sensitive
- Intimidating
- Not enough

Our emotions are the fragrance of our heart. Our heart reveals the disposition of our faith, and our faith is professed through our words. We are woven together from the time we were born, but we can become unraveled. It is by our salvation and through our transformation that we are woven back together.

The Lie: I am not enough - the Internal Processor

The person who believes they are not enough is really a gifted Internal Processor that has gone through trauma. Thoughts and emotions of feeling not enough will look like: thinking you don't matter because they carry the weight of everything, feeling inferior to others, struggling with insistent anxiety or comparison. Sometimes they focus only on the result of something rather than the process of what is asked.

A transformed Internal Processor is a person who takes time to carefully weigh everything. They will stand in the background with humble confidence and quietly process with a clear and organized idea of what is ahead. They will develop ideas internally and come back in their own time to deliver a profound solution. For the internal processor to be heard, they will need to communicate openly in their requirement for time and patience.

God has woven an Internal Processor to be a person that slows the quick down, discerning every situation with care and obedience. They will have beautiful and purposeful plans and solutions from standing in the waiting for God. Their execution and delivery is profound and intentional. They are great disciple makers, working one on one in personal relationships. They can also be great teachers if given space to plan. A biblical example of an Internal Processor would be John.

The Lie: I am too much - the Passionate Pursuer

The person that believes they are too much, is really the Passionate Pursuer who has been silenced and shut down by others. The thoughts and emotions of feeling too much will look like: being told to calm down, labeled dramatic, or overwhelming. They may have been told to be quiet because they are excessive, or talk too much. Often those who have been told they are too much will feel they have been skipped over, rejected, or left behind.

A transformed Passionate Pursuer is a person whose imagination and intensity are a gift. Their hunger is driven by an excitement for problem solving. They come across very independent, but it is because of their innate ability to absorb a situation quickly, analyze at a fast rate with much curiosity and imagination, then execute quickly. The beautiful nature of a Passionate Pursuer is their ability to be deeply empathetic and have strong emotional attachments to everything.

God has woven the Passionate Pursuer to be a person who moves others with great sentiment, tapping into every sense and emotion God has given us. Often in the Spirit, they will stir the masses with great execution toward Christ and the gospel. A Passionate Pursuer has the ability to impact a large group quickly when God stirs them, but often do not have the space for deeper one on one relational time. They make great evangelists, moving the masses. They are effective in ministry if given room to operate without inhibition. A biblical example of a Passionate Pursuer is Paul.

The wounded - the Burden Bearer

A wounded Burden Bearer is one that has been told they are too sensitive and over emotional and will have been deemed the scapegoat. They have been ridiculed, rebuked, and carry every negative label put on them. They are often misunderstood and sometimes explosive, and, as a result, will inevitably end up hiding in isolation. If not isolating, they will always be the mediator or fixer of everything—a peace keeper.

A transformed Burden Bearer is a person who is extremely sensitive to what others are facing. And, when given opportunity, will share the burdens of those who have been turned down as inconvenient. They have the innate and natural ability to hear and see things through vision, dreams, and the voice of God, feeling every message given to them through all the senses of sight, sound, touch and taste. They will stand in truth at the cost of their own life.

God has woven the Burden Bearer to be a person who will do all the things Jesus did, and they are aware of what people are facing and will be given a mission to transform them through intercession, scripture, and visions. They are called to share in the burdens of others no matter who they are, what they have done, or haven't done. They bless communities with their response to the Holy Spirit. They make great visionaries and prophets, carrying out the message of God. They will know great and mighty things. A biblical example of a Burden Bearer is Jeremiah the Prophet.

It is possible to relate to more than one of these. God moves us uniquely as we grow and mature in Him. Through *your* transformation in Christ, with healing and growth you will learn to materialize every word, truth, and moment with Him. You will carry out the message in the gift of who you are in Him. Which is ALWAYS enough and never too much.

BE AUTHENTICALLY unapologetic in Christ!

> *"You'll know them by the obvious fruit of their lives and*
> *ministries." Matthew 7:20*

We are a marked people. This means we are called to be authentically unapologetic about who we are in Christ. We will be known by our love, our faith, our forgiveness, and our steadfast hope for all things, living our lives with open and honest commitment and confession that Jesus is our savior!

God has freed us from ourselves to have a powerful voice, to speak the truth in public, and remain a follower when no one is looking. No hesitation, no distraction—you are in Christ without ceasing. He never said it would be easy. He said it would be rewarding. It says in 1 Corinthians 12:7 *"Each believer is given continuous revelation by the Holy Spirit to benefit not just himself but all."*

He has given each of us the confidence to come alive in Him. We need to allow the unique, awkward, uncomfortable, and often unpredictable side of Him to come in. Not fronts, no searching to impress, and no masks!

God is not here to punish or judge you, *"God did not send his Son into the world to judge and condemn the world, but to be its Savior and rescue it!"* John 3:17

God is not your score keeper. He is a loving and relational Father that has proven to continuously show up for us in all our failures.

God is not a legal system or religious duty manager. We all have free will. We are driven to love Him with all our heart and soul and mind, surrendering to His very voice from a place of gratitude and mercy, because he first loved us.

To gain the understanding of what being authentic in Christ is, you must grasp His love for you. Invite Him in, be baptized, and dedicate the rest of your life by immersing yourself into all He has in store for you.

I have learned so much about myself by being called into places where I did not think I was able. Every moment of every day is an opportunity to experience the love of Jesus and His people. *"For your very lives are our 'letters of recommendation,' permanently engraved on our hearts, recognized and ready by everybody."* 2 Corinthians 3:2

Rise up! Everything you say and do, everyone you meet, and everywhere you go, live your life walking in truth!

---

1. Do you identify with being too much? Not enough? Or wounded burden bearer? If so, please write down the reasons.

2. Look at the descriptions of a transformed and healthy emotional burden bearer, passionate pursuer, or internal processor. Do you identify with these? Cross out the negative reasons you wrote earlier, and write a prayer for yourself, staking claim to your emotions. Invite the Holy Spirit in, partner with all your emotions, and give thanks for the freedom to walk in them!

3. Write a declaration of your authentic self in Christ, then read it to your empowerment team! Ask them to pray with you and agree to keeping you in alignment with all things that WALK IN TRUTH!

NOTE TO READERS

Thank you so much for reading *Leaving The Lie,* a very vulnerable account of my life and a short teaching on how you can walk in your own truth.

Please leave a review or testimony. Your feedback matters. Honest reviews are welcomed.

If you found typos, grammatical errors, or something that needs addressing, please let me know! LeavingTheLieBook@gmail.com

Point your phone camera here to go to the *Leaving The Lie* Amazon review page.

We travel for teaching and/or speaking engagements and have availability for online or in-person meetings. Please contact us at contact@revivALL.org for more information.

ACKNOWLEDGMENTS

To my husband, Cody Davis: "My husband, I am deeply grateful for you. I would not be possible without God and you. The covenant team of a lifetime! You have been the prayer warrior, the patient pursuer of my heart as I went through triggers, journeying in and out of the stories once again. You are unwavering in support, advice, hugs, and kindness. Thank you for your obedience as a husband and taking the reins on what it means to kick generational junk in the butt! I love you, forever yours. A love as strong as death."

To my Kids: "I was asked what I thought about my kids reading some of the vulnerable places in my life. The truth is, a part of my life was difficult, and I had things done to me. I also did things I am not proud of. It is difficult to think about, but I imagine my daughters reading it and seeing me, not only as their mother, but a relatable woman who survived herself and others by finding Jesus. Looking at me now, they can see that God is the only way into living a whole, healed, and purposeful life. May the vulnerability of my story bring all my children and theirs a legacy of freedom."

To my Parents: "A part of my journey to health is to acknowledge that, while we all make large mistakes in our children's lives go to bed every night ridden with guilt, we know without a doubt that we have done the very best with what we were given. We love unconditionally, and with every one thing we failed, we rose up in a hundred good ways to make it right. I say "we" because I wouldn't know how to rise up without you leading the way. Thank you."

To those who have supported: "I would like to thank all those who have given so much to make this book happen, whether it was financially, emotionally, or prayerfully supporting me. You all have given me the encouragement I needed to press in and keep going. Kim Scott, Betty Cain, Judy Arnold, Victoria Robbins, Nancy Foreit, the Baileys, and many others. When I wanted to give up or I doubted myself, you all came through for me. Thank you to those who listened to me read, and those who walked me through the editing stages, specifically Dave Mundt and Kelly Kenyon. There are many others. I hold you close to my heart. And, my very best friend Ashley Atkins, for the endless number of phone calls keeping me going, prayers for my family and wisdom for our marriage, for truly seeing me inside and out. You are the best parts of me and the continuum to my joy and laughter."

RESOURCES

- DV Hotline, National Domestic Violence Hotline 1-800-799-7233
- One Safe Place Redding, CA 530-244-0117
- Suicide Hotline Suicide and Crisis Hotline, 988
- Dunamis Wellness, Neurofeedback Jennifer Bettes 530-338-0087
- Doug Porter LMFT, 530-244-7408
- Truth Ministries (Judy, Nancy, Victoria), www.truthministriesca.com
- The Stirring, 2250 Church Creek, Redding, CA, www.thestirring.org
- YWAM Chico, www.ywamchico.org
- Emerge, www.thestirring.org IG: @emerge_intensive
- Celebrate Recovery www.celebraterecovery.com

NOTES

1. The Lie: It Never Happened

1. Psychiatry.org, Diagnostic and Statistical Manual of Mental Disorders.

4. The Lie: I Am Unseen

1. Ncbi.nlm.nih.gov, effects of oxytocin, stress and sex.
2. Nida.nih.gov, MDMA DrugFacts, effects of Ecstasy.

6. The Lie: It Doesn't Matter - Part 2

1. www.thehotline.org, all information, references and recourses on abuse can be found here. Also, refer to www.domesticviolence.org

11. The Lie: I Am Too Much

1. Diagnosis definitions found at, APA Dictionary of Psychology.

ABOUT THE AUTHOR

When my children turn 18, I turn to the storage and pull out their memory box. Going through all their journals, school projects, pictures, and old stuffed animals. It is always something to look forward to. When my fourth child turned 18, we pulled out a table and set up a sifting station.

I was prepared for dusting off items, laughing at old childhood journals and crying over memories of childhood that have passed us by. I was not prepared for the internal pain that came welling up from the reminders and memories of the abuse I had endured. I was becoming increasingly angry, snapping at the kids, and crying for no apparent reason.

My chest started to hurt; my heart rate was increasing, I was triggered. I walked away to catch my breath; I could hear my family in the distance still crying out with cheerful excitement at every piece of memory.

I looked up into the sky and asked the Lord to relieve me of it. A gush of wind hit me, and God whispered, "burn the lie" and then He left. I took a deep breath and turned back to my family.

I wasn't living in a lie; I had left it all behind, but I had packed it all away and put it in storage. Holding onto a maybe or what if.

My fourth child turning 18 meant all I had gone through was over now. She was an adult, and I no longer had to be afraid.

I moved through the tables, pushing myself past all the memories and headed to the very back of the storage unit. It was dark and musty. I turned on my flashlight and found several heavy and very large totes, I began to pull them off one by one. At the bottom of the pile, in the very back of the storage unit was a black brief case with two locks.

Inside the brief case was every lie. I had held onto the idea that the abuser might come back at any moment and steal, kill, or destroy. Every note, every journal, every text, and every court document were waiting for his arrival.

Together, my husband and I pulled it out and unlocked its contents. We set it out in the middle of our yard, poured gasoline on it and set it ablaze. I watched as every piece burn away, ashes of lies, pain, fear and trauma lifted into the Heavens.

Today, my children get to experience the harvest of my growth. My daily prayer is that they encounter God in their own way and that the transformation of my live brings them faith and gives a new generation of hope.

Cody and I continue a ministry of love unconditional, with open hearts and minds for the One who died for it all. Speaking into the hearts of every person and making room up front at the table for those who stand in the back.

Cody mentors men and raises them up in trade that is pursuant to a business that runs from the heartbeat of God. I am a transformational coach and travel for motivational speaking engagements, breaking old patterns and guiding others into obtaining a confident and healthy life after trauma.

Together, my husband and I, are powerful intercessors. We gather to worship and intercede with compassion for the seemingly unseen. Bringing with us, a heart of family, compassion, and enthusiasm for life.

Our blessings come in the form of vindication, God's promise to freedom came with a vengeance and it looks like MERCY and COMPASSION. A person's unchanged circumstance in life can be an obstacle and they stop fighting for their own life.

Together we are healed and given a purpose to fulfill. Bringing the unique and divided together, making room for their gifts by setting a place at the table and inviting them into the body of community if they continue to deny the seat.

Our ministry remains in the Spirit, knowing the Spirit can and will agitate. We stand steadfast and strong with humble confidence, never backing out and pressing into His people with concern and honor. God is the supernatural defender, and we are the vessel.

We continue to take our ministry on the road, bringing transformation and testimony across the land in hope to bring us all together on...

ONE PATH. ONE PASSION.

www.revivALL.org
Instagram: @Davisrevivall and @Leaving_The_Lie
Contact: contact@reivall.org or leavingtheliebook@gmail.com

 instagram.com/Davisrevivall